Letters to Apple

Letters to Apple

The Memoire of an American in a Caracas Jail

A Story of Love and Adventure

by Leonard Ira Axelrad

Compiled by Anné Linden

Epigraph Books
Rhinebeck, New York

Paperback ISBN: 978-1-944037-92-5

eBook ISBN: 978-1-944037-93-2

Library of Congress Control Number: 2018931140

Book design by Colin Rolfe

Epigraph Books

22 East Market Street, Suite 304

Rhinebeck, New York 12572

(845) 876-4861

www.EpigraphPS.com

Dedicated with love to
Raven-Wolf

By Way of Introduction

Lenny (Axe) was in Venezuela to develop an option he had on land on the island of Margarita off the coast of Caracas. He applied to the Venezuela government for incorporation of his company. In the U.S. it takes a week or two to incorporate. In Venezuela it can take much longer. After waiting months, Lenny started raising money for the project before his incorporation was fully completed. One of the investors realized the company was not yet incorporated and lodged a complaint against Lenny. The situation was explained, the money was returned to the investor and he withdrew the complaint.

Whenever a legal complaint is made against a foreigner in Venezuela his/her name is put on a list at the airport customs office. Because of bureaucratic red tape Lenny's name had not been removed. On his way home for Thanksgiving he was stopped by Interpol before boarding his plane. Nothing was explained to him. He was treated roughly and probably did not respond with the respect those officials felt due them. They threw him in jail and his plane landed in Kennedy International Airport without him.

Lenny finally did get out of jail and brought himself and five notebooks home filled with handwritten letters and drawings. When he died two years later, I thought they would be part of his legacy to his son, so I organized and typed them, cried a lot, put them away and began to get on with my life.

In 2017 I was going through some old papers when I came upon these letters. After rereading them with much nostalgia and tears, I realized this story is timeless and worth sharing; and so I decided to publish this book. The unconditional love I received from this man over the three years we were together has made the difference that makes the difference in my life since.

"Apple"
Anné Linden

Wednesday. Sleepless night…up early…plenty of time…nervous, thinking of you…love…sex…et al. Lenny-Apple and more; so as I ponder -- thru the gate -- wait -- what now? Me! Oh boy, so here we go! Missed the plane -- tell 'em I'll be back, okay…sure! Off in a 4-wheel drive -- young guys nice, not like the stoppers who wouldn't talk. Arrive at special office…wait…no speaks de Spanish. Oh, my Apple… she's waiting…I'm yearning; she's pissed -- me too. Can I make a call? Sit down -- no nothing. Hours go by…talk to young guy…he's been in States. Oh no, here we go to the city…now here's the place, Interpol, and it starts…one question…a thousand, and I don't know so on the go. Still no call to friend or aide. No Apple. The plane…my plane has arrived… no me. Oh, I'm sorry, I send you kisses and all, don't leave me…love me & understand. I can't reach you 'cept thru my heart and head…hear me: I love ya, don't go away mad…later she'll be scared…still no calls.

At last my friend is called -- too late for today -- finally got through to him in evening. He said he'd call you.

Please understand & don't worry…I'll do that! I'll be coming soon. Sure -- Sure. Sit down…more forms…translation. They think I'm a liar. You're reached and all's well -- you know & now you're back on my side. Funny how the wheels turn…180°. No trouble…mad…trouble…sad. Oh my love…hear me: I love ya…you're my Apple and all. Whatdayaknow…

Ali fights tonight. Sit around and watch it with the boys (nice guys) --
with their irons and fast moves. Like 'em but they can't figure me out,
know that means zilch -- so what! You know, all day long I worried...
Tried so hard...stone wall...no food...stomach crazy...pee every second
minute...searched, fingerprinted, now testimony all done. No -- more of
same. Now slate-eyed doing a job...Big Boss goes home. Sleepless nite...
thinks about you...send you messages...get 'em...you're all I want. What
the fuck is going on? Sleep (ha) on short couch...shades of college...no
reading matter: one newspaper & my papers -- tell ya later. (Tried to flush
everything down the toilet) Some trip! Lasted all nite...to bathroom and
back...with pangs and no love...all alone. Guns and heavies all around...
teach me Spanish, with a smile...me too in reverse. Next morning friend
comes...all well; they say home today. No, not yet! More reports...ques-
tions. Tired...no food...drink water...can't eat when I try. Better that
way...skinny Lenny...Apple Like...good! Loves ya...the bestest. Boy, are
you crazy...I feel it, but now I outcrazied you! Some way to go! Everyone's
gone -- tomorrow I'll go -- I hope. Will travel all day to get to you...hope
I make it in time. You're mine...don't go...you must know...I love ya! I'm
coming, you too...soon my love love love, and then tomorrow will come.
But now I think...39...life begins again. new start for me and you...don't
forget it...you can't outrun Lucky Lenny Love...too much going for us. I
wonder what'll happen next? It's like I just got out of high school and life
turns round again. New directions -- wonder if I'm going the right way?
Not much time left in life. All eternity...in a second. All things seem to
be working against me, but you know, in my exhaustion, I somehow am
feeling stronger. Know what it is...you, my love...feel my strength...I'm
coming...it's yours...come again. It's me and you and you and me forever
and ever more. Tonight I wait for tomorrow and wonder if I'll leave. I even
prayed for me and for you. Wherever it is, it's together, no more alone...
even now. But what frustration, help me-- I love you & I'll take care of you.

Boy, some trip for you! Well, that's what my life and yours is…some trip! The tripsters are all here. Now hear this…I love you. Until tomorrow. I'm yours…Love Apple Me.

≡

Tomorrow here, Thanksgiving, slept four hours…music…dad a dad a da; dad a dad a dad ah dah…wait for 7…call airport (only one allowed) and make reservations. Puerto Rico to New York or Miami to New York? Hope I get to plane at 4 -- could be home in five hours. God, how I miss you.

Funny and weird afterthoughts: on way to airport Tuesday it was 33 Bs. for cab (my number) -- then in airport my lucky butterfly chain broke and then 1-2 hours after they stopped me at Customs and you know what happened. Ah, yes…15 more minutes to go to see if I get a plane connection…gotta get home today. Thanksgiving, Thanks God…Thanks Apple…Thanks All! We see later.

Almost 12…more fingerprinting…still no answer. Big man doesn't talk. Feel weird, bored…reading Nikon book…did some notes, drawing. There's no other reading material and my clothes damp, underwear ridiculous. Get lucky Lucky Lenny. Thought for now: is holiday in States preventing my getting info here today and they may also check passport, if that's by mail I'll be here a week! Some fun. I miss you. I hope I get out of here today. Lunch here 12-3 and then only three hours to get info, and then another night here and so on. Boy, some spot, need you here in private room, big bed and all's well that ends mit the Axe and the Apple…I love ya, Lenny.

≡

Well, I'm now in prison and yesterday was a holiday, so no word from States that my passport okay. Came in afternoon, it's the worst place in Caracas. A 220 pound wrestler and another cat (my cell-mates), both 33, and in room 33. The lottery number today was 33 and there's 33 all over -- it's a signifier!! Room is 10' by 6'…three people… but not rectangular…so my feet are on the toilet. Sleep on stone floor on paper…it's cold…food bad…can't eat…heart pounding, nervous and tranquil, hot and cold…reading Spanish newspapers aloud and learning Spanish from my cellmates.

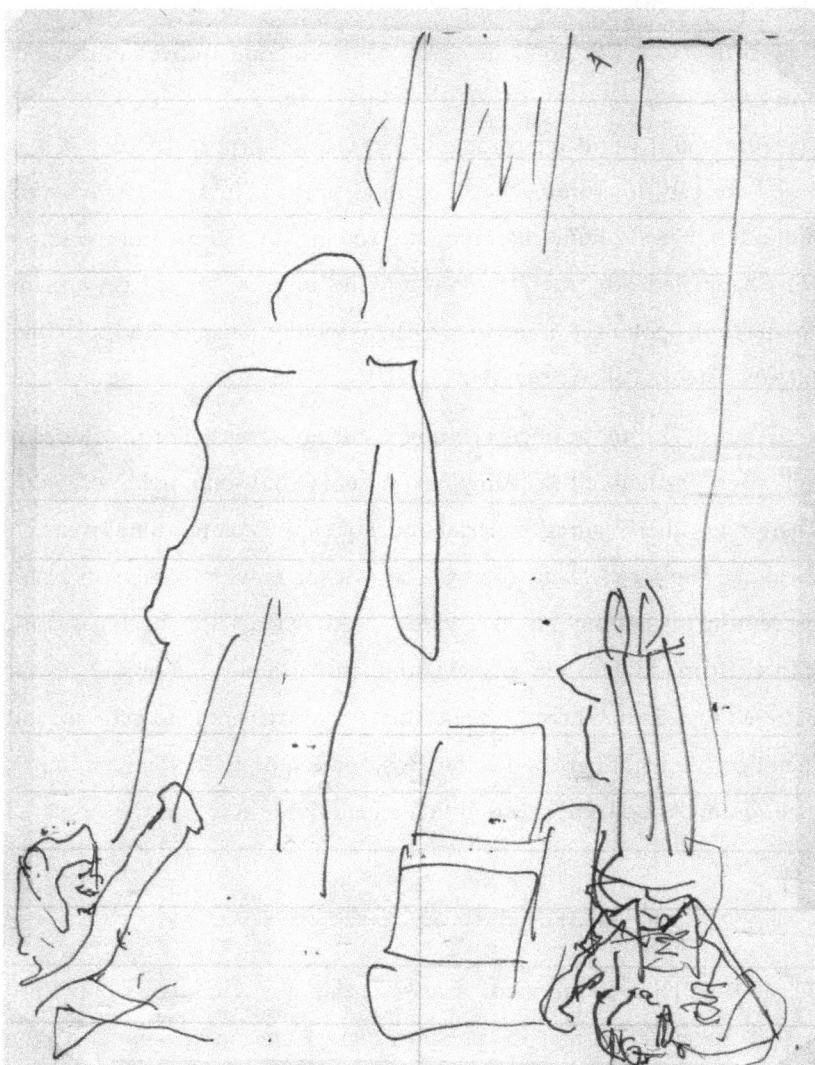

Friend Arthur comes today with lawyer. Here guilty 'til innocent proven. Have decided omens against me here in Venezuela & must pack and leave for good when they let me out of jail. Crazy to stick with it…miss you and the thought of you keeps me together. Well, they say 40 is a new life and I'm going to have one! Could be here 1 - 7 days. It's dangerous to go in corridor -- bumping off 2 - 3 dead a week. Dangerous people but I seem to be okay. An American came down and talked to me. I told him about my heart and he'll try to get me moved in to a better section.

Guys in cell very nice but can't have anything here cause people will kill you for it. Left baggage and camera at Interpol with detective who spoke French…said he'd give it to Arthur. I believe him. So just have my clothes, this pad, two magazines, *Hot Rod* and *Mad* and some cigarettes. Man, it's crazy! As I said, I'm lucky with my roommates. There's all kinds here: rapists, murderers, etc., all very dangerous. We stay locked in. I want to take a shower but they said no go, so back to hand body washing…that and killing time 'till I get out…reminds me of the hospital. I was lucky: they didn't beat me up and they let me make a call the first day. Was told sometimes it takes a week before you can get one out. Well, American's due back at one, he'll maybe get me transferred to a better section with him. He knows Spanish and is groovy, also knows name of consul and American ambassador so can maybe expedite things. Hope so…miss you…love you. This writing helps as I can't sleep. The floor's cold and my belt loops dig into my back; can't lie on sides cause my bones dig into floor. Well, hope I get out or that a transfer is to a better place. Boy oh boy -- do you think there's a message here? Yes! Time for a change. Just me and you…Off in the wild blue yonder…together. Love ya…tell ya later. Come here…I want to show you something! Remember shades of Florida and stone floor of Arembepe! Well love, sign me in at your place, I've had it here! Love ya…see ya soon I hope. Now I wait till one when American, his name's Todd, comes back and maybe he can do something, also Arthur comes with attorney and I feel ya praying for me. Kiss the kids and Duggie and Sam and kittens and cats. Love Lucky Lenny. I'm alive and not so well in Venezuela.

Went to eat: some scene…line up…fast trays…all sit down…eat fast. Bread, 2 liquid bowls, a one inch slice of meat, had the coffee and at a signal you file out fast. The sound of tin bowls dropping…clank clank clank…1 or 2 a second and then the trays, and you file out finished or not. We three cell mates come in at end -- the last line and least time to eat. It's okay for just walking out, otherwise stay in cell…dangerous outside… people all hit on me for cigarettes and I have to give it to them. Looks like I could take all but a few -- except for weapons -- but have no eyes.

Saw lawyer -- see judge on Monday (hope) and then out. It's Friday dammit, otherwise tomorrow…that's life…take it as it comes. Gave lawyer my necklace and ring and belt -- now have only same clothes and cigarettes (four packs a day). He says Monday -- Judge -- then out. Complaint withdrawn. Back to room. After lunch Ernie, Todd's friend, came by with big bowl of onion soup and said I'm going over to his castle at 6 o'clock where there's a personal shower, bed, etc. The chief guard said same at lunch (tonight or tomorrow -- hope soon). Now Todd came by and said same thing. Heart feels funny…sure, wouldn't yours? So now it is looking up a bit and Todd knows the ropes. I'll help him if I can with my lawyer but he seems connected. Hope so! I'm sure I'll move -- my lawyer requested same so hope to stay okay for the next few days. It's like the hospital, when you don't know what'll happen or if you'll die. So we all die…It's the way you live that counts. "Qui Vivra Virra --" "He who lives, will see." But you can bet I'm Lucky Lenny & I'll be with you soon my Love -- I'm coming home baby -- dad a dad a -- dah dah dah da. Just heard that Jesus died at 33. Well, I've reversed the process & I'll start to live with a smile when I get to you. Apple got her arms all around me, no evil thoughts can harm me for I thank God I'm in her arms.

These Guys don't read, so light is out (naked bulb) & room is dark. They don't shit either (2 days -- nothing), not so the Axe! Hope I go to the other section, but it's 5 or 6 now & who knows! Ernie just here and gave me candy & 2 Bs. change -- he said he'll bring me magazines & ask again -- hope so! Visitor's day tomorrow -- once a week only in this block, and then only 10 - 15 minutaws (I forget how to spell here), and it's hard to write in the dark. Light is on now with paper in front of the bulb, like a Butterfly. Nites cool & damp…belting makes a hole in my back and is bad for cyst which is swollen. I just ripped lining of belt up & out, it's better… but boy is floor hard and cold. The newspaper helped but not enuf - pouring now and mail call or something I don't know what is out there in hall -- it's like the jungle, but I'm okay…just paranoid I guess. But so is my wrestler roomie…we stay behind the locked door…only person who can cut you is in your cell & it's okay here, Thank God. Could be weird…they jump you…kick the shit out of you & rob you. Not so me, but then I don't know how I look to them! It's like I'm a kid again, thinking people are jibbing me but not sure -- paranoia for sure -- but that's what not knowing the language does. They speak & laugh & you think it's at you but you're not sure and sometimes it's so…just cause you don't understand the inside joke. Oh well, I should care…that's not my problem, it's my body & my mind & I can't sleep…thoughts flashing…body aching & yearning for you only…you're my Love…I'm Coming!

They sleep but I don't now and I'll never do so at nite when dark is dark & can't stretch my legs cause toilet in the way. Lying on my side is out because thigh joint bone is bruised & if I lie on stomach my ribs get it. Oh well, hard floor is good for back. When I leave I'll be poifecto…ho ho… when's that? I hope before I get used to this. Some guys here on floor 20 - 30 years…wow…do we have a lot to be thankful for. Watch me…Thank You, Thank You for being in my life, My Love!!!!

One guy talks & talks & my friend the wrestler hates it, but he's here & boy is he crazy. Across the hall there are 8 guys who raped one girl with a knife at her throat and they got caught. Also murderers, knifers, muggers, robbers, et al; so I don't have it so bad…hope I move tonite tho, but who knows what's there…we'll see. Chain smoking -- 4 packs a day -- wish I had my cigars, et al! Lights off -- power out -- on again for 10 minutes -- off again -- now on 1 hour later -- that's how it is here. Underwear is green. My cyst stopped bleeding now and I'm thankful for that.

Boy, do I miss you & everybody & dogs & cats & home…home. "Home is where the heart is" -- that's you for me…where I wanna be alla time…mit you, can't stop thinking about you.

Yells all the time in the hall…God knows what they're saying. Queens roaming all over: one beautiful one I thought was a girl…she's/ he's nice, but oh no keep away…they all have blades. Paranoia again, you said it -- I hope I get this out with me -- I have to carry everything with me if I leave room or else it's stolen. How's that for travelling light? Don't want to rest -- afraid I won't sleep tonight -- it's hot & stuffy & humid after the rain. Took off my shirt and get more looks from roamers in corridor who look in thru door bars. I'm getting' in shape…stomach flat… haven't really eaten or slept in years it seems. The heart-on I have is only for you & our freedom together; funny to think of freedom as together but it's right on & I sure know that's the way HOME -- "Where the Heart is - YOU"!!

Wearing glasses too much, but now writing so I don't use them and exercising -- I forgot about the pain for awhile! My back & chest killing me!! Hope you had Thanksgiving Dinner…I sure felt you here…some Holiday, but, "THIS TOO SHALL PASS"!

And so on & so on, as life flows thru me I really start feeling more in control of myself…as if the anguish produces its own strength. Wonder if I'll get my camera & bag & AMX checks back…think so. He was a nice detective cat…23…strong & a girl chaser & was most sympathetic, 9 to 1 for it…but who knows…?

My shoulder mate just yelled out something out into the hall, the 'craszy'…who knows what he said. They all just scream out…to no one in particular…some Scene! Pain is back again…flashes in & out…never get comfortable. Three guys in a space across less than our bed -- can feel the breathing of guy next to me on my shoulder.

When's the move to the other place? There's a bed there…I might sleep. But it's only 6 or 7 now & nothing happens when they say here, they just say okay, okay and walk away -- cute? A lot of talk & nothing happens…just waiting & waiting. Time passes like a leaf falling from heaven, but it never lands at a point on earth & here the floating is hot & streaming & hell -- hell is where the frenzy is & that's what's happening here.

So, I'll think of you again…that's heaven…in your arms…thighs…lips…in you…on you…I love you…Len…

Well, I'm still here, hard floor and all, tomorrow is visitor's day & hopefully I move to a bed. Just got a blanket & 2 books (in English) from a guy I met while being fingerprinted at the Secret Police place. I gave him a few cigarettes there, and he recognized me -- calls me "My Frand" -- (I didn't talk at first here to anyone on advice from my wrestler cellmate, who's my Professor de Spanish, somehow I understand about ¼ of what he says…good cat…looks after me and keeps to his own).

Now floors warm & maybe I'll sleep a little tonight…need pants without seams to sleep on the floor because otherwise they put holes in your bones -- get ready here's a bone in your hole, I'm a comin' home babe! Anyhow, it's better now, & the queens keep making the rounds, doing errands & buying cigarettes…coffee…etc. The boys here kid me because they (the queens) keep hitting on me --'rest tranquilla' -- it's only you I'm thinkin' on -- but it's okay, you just smile & jive with everybody.

There's a 4th Guy here now & he'll sleep sideways near door with feet doubled up under the sink -- God knows why he's here. Anyhow, the clown in the middle next to me keeps giggling & talking like Gonzales Gonzales (The Mexican Outlaw in Treasure of Sierra Madre) They took him -- my new cell mate -- while he was sleeping; he woke up with hands & irons on him -- (wrote bum checks in his company)…a Nutso! My ashtray is a milk container & my pillow an Ajax Plastic-like bottle with paper on it & Hot Rod Magazine over it. Mad is my other reading matter -- just got another Mad from "My Frand" -- & a girlie book type comic in Spanish…thought it was in English at first. Maybe he's straight -- he's here for kicking the shit out of somebody somewhere, but everybody's been kool (that's my cigarette brand here) with me so far & I hope it keeps up. So my bed (ha) is hot now…but it's softer on my back & a better pillow on top of my Ajax-type Jap neck roll. Would you believe it -- 4 days since I started to you -- I miss you terribly, Love You…

4 days & believe it or not I'm beginning to understand & speak a little Spanish (wow, what a way to learn)! Hope I go to other building tomorrow…it's really crowded here -- boy am I gonna crowd you Apple!

My wrestler friend says he's thinking about his kids alla time (wants me to meet his wife tomorrow & write me in N.Y.). A good Kat (accused of taking about $25 of clothes) -- he'll be here about 2 - 3 weeks before they'll tell him who accused him; he works & seems strong mentally, an Aquarian with good smile & strong as Hell. He says me & him can keep ourselves cool against any physical things easy, but he doesn't want to get cut to beat up somebody -- (Me Tambien). The craszy's got 7 kids…the guy keeps giggling about fucking & is Nutso but okay, considering he's sleeping 2" from my left shoulder and doesn't shut up, a Virgo. The other guy's thin & okay looking…been here 3 days…I still don't know why, Boy "conyo" is a word like fucker in English -- means Cunt. Every other sentence an expletive like Boy or Gosh or Shit or whatever you want. But I want your Conyo or whatever else you have…you've got alla me, except I'm here & you're there…but I'm with you & I feel you sending me messages. God, I hope you're okay & haven't flipped yet…I'm coming Apple…Axe…By the way the last thing I got at Interpol was an Apple but I couldn't eat it cause it ain't like you…I miss ya…I'm coming! Will read again or bullshit… it's 9:30, & 3 hours to kill, then I hope I can sleep. I'll pick up later…Len! Loves the Apple & the APPLEAXE! That's US…Later & Now & Forever… (Me (n) U)…

Next morning comes; talked last nite for 2 - 3 hours and made my-self understood & understood about ½ of what was said to me -- (HA!) Read a little & then went to sleep for 2 hours…smoked 10 cig-arettes for 2 hours & tossed for 2. Then a huge commotion of beating on metal…no one knew if someone was getting killed or not, turned out to be reveille (some trick, huh) -- jumped up -- heart beating when I heard it so I'm really exhausted this morning. Wanted to take a shit but I'm the only one who does in this place so will wait until after breakfast. Anoth-er commotion -- tins banging -- screams & yells. Had 5 sips of gruel & a sip of cold water coffee -- ugh -- then back to cell 33. Wrestler demanded cleanup & he did most of it…good kat! Now laying down writing…go-ing to toilet soon. The craszy is sitting on it with his pants on (no seat) -- everybody's on his own & you have to exert yourself on others & tell them not to fuck around. It'll be cooler now & I'll probably leave here for the other place & have to start all over again. (Hope Arthur spoke to you & you're not too fucked up behind all this -- love ya!) Going to depose the Craszy & take a shit & wash body…still haven't taken a shower…will wait until other place or until I get out of here; then read (half of Mad

left yet) & then maybe visitors. "Well here goes…book down…hide it…
all my things are easily put on my person…traveling light! Speak to you
soon I hope…Love Love Love Ya. Here I Go…Axe…Just heard a dog
bark. Probably the one I saw last night out window on ground floor,
flashed on Duggie & Sam & Kittens & You…miss you…soon…soon…
my love -- I hope I hope I hope…

========================

Saturday. Well it's morning…went to the mess hall (for the exercise)
-- it's safer than staying in cell alone, carrying all I have except books
& blanket. Came back & went out in yard to wait for visitors. Everybody
goes…it's like animals on parade…walking up & down. My wrestler
friend introduced me to his family & they asked me what I needed. The
crazsy --(he's here for a year) had no visitors (although he's got 7 kids), &
the new guy (care theft) had no visitor. No older guys here (several exceptions) & the other thing is I'm the only one here I've seen with glasses
although I don't wear 'em outside cell. Waited till 10:30 -- nobody & then
lawyer showed. Said I'll be out by Friday -- which is what they said at
Interpol when they brought me here -- (7 days for investigation). Lawyer
said I'll get transferred Monday cause the Chief of the Section isn't here
on weekend. I told him Todd said ditto but he played it down as to Todd
having any influence & said only his word had effected the transfer. I went
along with his note, but don't know. I hope he's heavy enough -- wants
500 Bs. for Monday & then some -- (seems too little for the holdup action
that goes on down here, but again who knows?) He said he expected my
friend Arthur to call Friday afternoon so he didn't take care of the transfer
then as he was stuck in his office waiting for the call (which never came).
Somebody's full of Shit…I asked him if we had his home number & he
said he had none (sounds like a lightweight to me). Todd's got a heavy he
says who cares not what you did (Murderers out for $2,000 the next day).

Hope that I don't get locked in with the lightweight lawyer -- although all lawyers build up their task to build up their fees…We'll See!

Back out to the yard -- had been talking to lawyer just inside of gate cause he's afraid he'll be contaminated or robbed in yard -- for sure he's afraid! So I'm out here waiting for my friend Arthur…it's about 12 noon and no Arthur…not like him…he's like a rock with appointments…never lets you down…something must be wrong…5 minutes left to visiting hours. No Arthur -- what's wrong? Told lawyer to call him. Heat's getting to me out here…sun bearing down on hot cement and people and noise. Feel faint…Pain in chest & arm suspicious…Maybe I'm worrying too much, ha, ha. Well…tomorrow…he can't come although someone told me now he can -- maybe they confused the days. Lawyers thought it was Sunday yesterday…oh, well, hang in there and hope my partner is okay. Well time's up. Here's a guy bearing in on me -- pronounces my name weirdly -- I say Americano -- he says follow him…

Arthur, beautiful Arthur showed & brought me other pants, tee shirt, underwear & lots of books. He said they searched him & wouldn't let him bring in a lot of stuff. He looks drawn…must be a hell of a strain on him, told me the news…told me to keep myself together, etc…& limped off with a hug & a smile. A good, good, guy & friend (stand up). Gave me details on events as they're going ahead. Said also it's out of Interpol's hands & now up to the Judge. Said you wanted to know why I didn't call Thanksgiving (me too! why don't they let you make any phone calls?...it's fucked up!) But I sure thought on you…I loves you you dopey beautiful loved - one-woman mine…Don't get your nutso suspicious bird working against us…I send you sweet & beautiful thoughts & lots & lots of love. You're near to me alla time…don't go chasing fake shadows…it's hard enuf living with the real items.

So anyhow now sitting here with my bundle & books…can't leave until the whole place goes into lunch -- we're last as this is our visitor's day

-- 2 hours in the sun…feel weak & faint & shitty. Forgot to tell Arthur to bring me my Nytro glycerine Pills…hope my body doesn't fuck up, but pains in chest & arm are worse. Some guy's talking to me & wrestler & carrying on non-stop. I gave him some money (2 Bs.) & cigarettes before at other place, but he's just being nice I guess (he's here for 4 years). Wish he'd shut up…I feel terrible. Well here we go (2 hours later). Up to eat -- ugh! I have some soup & a little bread but feel lousy. Finished eating in 5 minutes & speeded out to the tune of tins falling and trays banging into tin drums…Bang-Bang-Bang-Bang-Bang-Bang-2-3 a second and repeating for 5 - 10 minutes as some file out while others come in and are still eating…Some dinner music!

Back to the joint & clean up…throw out old underwear (out the bars into the yard)…put on new jeans…Thank Goodness! Reading & Todd shows…tells me he expected me but Chief didn't get to it yet -- the latest it should be is Monday, same story as lawyer so suspect it'll happen. He tries to get me a mattress & pills from one of the girls -- they're all in for murder except the pretty one (car theft). So I guess paranoia is well placed with them, although they run the concessions here…& certainly do the servicing…

No Go…it's the weekend (no Chief to make the transfer)…Todd come back before 6…the Chiefs here now are groovy -- he introduces me…they already know me and are all cool. I hit on them for my pills but need a doctor's order for it. The bugs, mosquitos & cockroaches are running & biting…they've really come out to say hello for the weekend!

Dinner's being served (we go first -- it's about 3). I'm hanging in here alone, locked in, fuck everything -- I'll take what comes. Whadayaknow -- the guy in the visitor's pen (works there) that I gave 2 Bs. for a mattress just came by to ask for another 2 Bs. I gave it to him but probably shouldn't have & he said tomorrow or Monday. I told him if I'm not here to give the mattress to the wrestler or come up & see me (hope I'm there!)

They're back already -- 10 minutes the most and the talky guy just asked for money -- I said don't have it & my roomie's eyes said "right on, don't give to NOO-Bodee"…So here we are again -- bugs biting, just rained - I'll stop for awhile. Was going to give this book to lawyer to give to Arthur but maybe Arthur'll come & it'll be better that way. I just don't want my thoughts stolen…"Par-a-Noi-Yaa," tell me who you rrrrR--?

I love ya, ya hear me? hang on I'm hanging in & the other things here are coming along okay so perhaps all will be alright soon. Certainly will be as soon as I have you in my arms…Soon, Soon, Love…

———————————

So, wadayaknowabout that, one of the Mariposa (girls) came by & for 5 Bs. plus 2 (I voluntarily tipped a Chief)…I've got an old lumpy-bumpy mattress (cotton ticking). It's about eleven…I've been reading & rapping and my back pain is receding as well as my inner head pain. I'm sure it's no surprise to you I do my best smiling, et al, on my back in a bed & that's what's happening. Just a little relief, a little comfort & my life seems to be going up hill again -- which probably means I'm getting adjusted to this bullshit existence & can face tomorrow with a better smile. No visitors in this section on Sunday. Now that I've got reading matter & my Spanish has improved to a point where I understand about 10 times more than ever, I can get around a little in my head without straining so much. I've got 3 new pads to write you on (U) (U) (U); which Basillo's wife (he's the wrestler) brought me along with cigarettes & soup & a container of Cara-bobo juice (like oranges), so I'm going into round 2 -- which will be when I move…hopefully Monday to Todd's Cliff…in this "House of Towers"….

I just fit my ass into one of the holes in the blanket, got my feet on the wall& my head on the toilet with my boots as a pillow. My pillow now is a plastic bag of my pants (brown Venezuelan) 2 pairs of underwear, socks & a tee shirt. My brown sport shirt has a label called Chutzpay (which we bought in Woodstock with the planes on it) -- it means "nervy Bastard." I watch all my things here because unless you got it on you it's 9 to 1 it's ripped off; although the odds are down now as everybody here is aware of me & they treat me with respect, which is wild as I'm tame next to the records here -- but you know Lucky Lenny. I think it's starting to come my way at least to the extent that I can think to Friday about getting out of here and not freaking out before I do. If you or I thought it was bad before, this is the World Series next to Sandlot Ball. It's funny but this is the beginning or end of my book with all the things I've thought & written maybe put in their Place in my Life's-Eye...

I mean you, & I can't believe it myself, but even everything I've been working on here: oh well the paradoxical human from one extreme to the other...that's for sure me...highly unstable & for sure volatile compound of flesh, emotions & spirit...just like everybody else I guess...but I'm coming on babe...mostly on you...or couldn't you feel it.

So, Luci came by -- she's the pretty one & is a barber & wants to cut my hair...I declined. She cut Todd's & friend today & is really very easy...not pressing like the others & I'm the reluctant "for real" virgin so I guess the unattainable (what's that?) attracts or is just lil ole me...yourself you know. SO GO KNOW & TELL ME!!!

Arthur even brought the toilet paper so I'm living because my insides are outside-up side downside...Anyhow, I feel the weight of momentum on my side (must be because it's Saturday nite & no movies). I wonder what you're doing & thinking...it better be of me or when I see ya soon in my new streamlined frame I'll up-fuck your body right off this earth to where the Cosmos is met when you & I unite...tonite...all-right...get ready here I come...back to you, but just let me take a toilet break again! You know what the amoebas are like here in the water -- well this here water ain't purified too good for sure & U know me -- Liquid Len.

So this is the place where I'm going to do my absolute fasting -- for real and plenty of rest if I could just get rid of the tension. Started out to you early but will get to you late, but we'll make up for it "real quick"! I'm doing my yoga! No one's hurt me except by limiting my mobility & I'm on my way back, don't let down I'll be there soon. The pains in my chest are better now but gotta check it out, maybe just the gas & I've got plenty of that -- & I know you've got the car! Time is all we've both got & that's what I know we'll learn how to spend in Chapter III of this Episode, entitled Me and You, et al, S.A., et al, & the New Life of AppleAxe Ensemble -- here, there or anywhere, just as long as we're together.

I'm gonna stop now as the 3 charmers are all snoring & the bugs are biting & I guess it's time cause this book's run out, but I've got 3 more for tomorrow & tomorrow & tomorrow sinks out & up in this petty pace (race) called Life.

Life is where the love is…that's U & Me…AppleAxe for sure!

Sunday here…it's a heavy visitor's day for the other Sections & heavy guards are on, altho this morning I saw Rohme (the tall and fearful chief -- Jefe) & Ismael (short chief) still on duty & they called me Senor Axe…

My neck which has felt like hell since the motorcycle accident feels a lot better…I've been doing the Yoga exercises & am getting good at cracking them thar bones. Last nite I read Newsweek & got several good points down for my book. It's all kindsa stuff that's not in print & I'm gonna give it a shot when I get past this hurdle. Boy what a difference a little ole mattress makes. Slept 4 - 5 hours & feel a little better but am real sluggish. I look forward to doing some real exercise…swimming, running etc. I've been doing a lot of breathing exercises but am having trouble since I've been smoking cigarettes like mad & my throat feels like a saw is in it. So with my new calm I'm cutting down to (1) pack a day & by the time I leave will not smoke at all (?)…but it's the only relaxer as of now. So anyhow last night I was talking to you a lot and we made all sorts of plans. I hope things work out here because the whole world is our play-pen & in spite of this experience, if all works out well, I think we'll be here in Venezuela. Anyway, I made myself come last nite with you & I hope you enjoyed it & got the message. That's something for here because it's been impossible up to now to even think in that direction (manually speaking) until I got my mattress & now with a blanket…I'm getting to know ya again…

Since my pillow is my clothes bag now, I gave the new guy, Herman, my toilet cleaner Ajax type bottle pillow. Went to breakfast for the walk & had some of this coffee that runs thru you like an irrigation system. The mess hall is just that -- & I'm popular cause I don't eat & give all the food away. Came back & took a nap & woke up to a lot of noise as visitors are coming for some of the guys here who are evidently under other jurisdictions. The guards scream out their names and they scream back! Barkers in the hall yell out what they're selling! A slight breeze -- I wonder how that happened?...Don't think lawyer will come today & I'm hanging in the rest of the day...may go to dinner at 3 - 4 for the 10 minute break & exercise, although I want to stay around so my stuff doesn't get ripped off till I get into other section (it's safer there I'm told). Am now memorizing the rest of the yoga exercises (Arthur brought my book) although I don't have enuf room to do it I look forward to that -- this place really makes me feel like I'm back in the hospital and I'm gonna die. Me, No Never Now...for sure...I've got a lot of things to do -- ouch, the bedbugs & mosquitos are biting again. Well it's all up to ourselves as to what our life trip is -- you see that dramatically here & you better believe that you & me is gonna have a good one. My Grandfather when he was dying said to me "I had a good one Lennyboy" & he was just a lil ole tailor. Money, that's the bug and it looks like this extended tour will fuck up my other income, but hopefully something here will turn up.

Was just thinking about my father & the last time I spoke to him when he asked me to "kill him" & I said, "we have to say goodbye" & he said "we've said goodbye all our lives -- kill me." I had the nurse give him a shot which relieved the pain & asked him if he was all right now -- he nodded yes & I left him with my mother & then kissed him Goodnight & Said "I love you Chiam Volf" & then the next day he was dead..."I love you, Chiam Volf" tears in eyes, hard guy. Guards in uniforms just came by screaming names into cells. You can't tell the guards by the scorecards as most of the time they don't look any different from the prisoners...no uniforms except for visitors day, so you have to be careful of what you say or they nail you. All sorts of stuff going on here -- but the sellers are all squealers to lighten their number -- all there is to do is keep to yourself & hope your cell mates are good guys cause that's where the exposure is. Well I'll read for awhile & see what happens next, that's the one thing about life…U never know what's gonna happen next -- for sure in here. War one second, peace next & then disaster & so on & so on & so on. But you're happening now and now is the only thing that's ever happening…I Love Ya…Lucky Len…Lucky Apple.

———————————

Reading the cartoon book that's in Spanish that turns out to be a Spanish-English book so I'm learning the slang of sex in Spanish. Mosquitos are biting & I'm licking the bites like a dog. Yep, no visitors. My wrestler friend just got a package of food again thru the bars. He hasn't shit yet -- just the craszy this morning -- 4 days without a shit can you believe it? I guess compared to the way he generally eats this is a fast; but boy a lot of farts in the room -- the breeze lets you know it! Writing on my back is hard, but it sure passes the time & I'm doing something I've not had the motion just the notion for…Writing. Wrestler's wife brought me another juice -- came in thru the bars, so I'm juicing it up -- that & the cigarettes…I can feel the nicotine & see that cigarettes give you a flash, especially with nothing in your system!

The garbage can is out the window and you should see what it looks like out there -- garbage and wall and barbed wire to keep the garbage inanimate and the humans inside.

Later and soon my love! There's a beating of jungle drums on our wall -- pretty good rhythm! I've finished 2 books, exercised again, smoke 2 cigarettes, about to hit one again. Going blind reading in this room which is dark during even hi daylight and now waiting for lunch (not to eat), but just to get out and walk for the 10 minutes it takes. It feels like it's midnight but it's probably only 1 or 2; we're late for lunch because of visiting I guess or whatnot. I'm getting out of this room -- don't give a shit if they steal everything. I take my glasses, pen and these notebooks -- guess it's called stircrazy and I sure feel it's vibes. Sunday always is mellow but here it's weird, a strange relaxed day and at the same time heavy cause of the traffic (visitors), and special uniformed hard guards. Wrestler's wife brought me more juice but he couldn't see her so I guess there is no visiting on Sunday for us. One thing here is that no matter what is said, no one is sure what's happening until it reveals itself! That's Life I guess, but boy am I a little nuts already! The writing helps and so does the books and mattress but what hurts is "no you" and no mobility to do whatever…claustrophobia metal and physical -- some drag. Think I'll start on something or other else but I'm restless and can't seem to hold to anything for a long time -- except the one thing that's keeping my writing and my head, heart and soul together --

I'm sure you're "out of your bird today." I can feel it and maybe it's you and maybe me zeroing in on each other's vibes that's doing it, so try to cool it and think "nice" of "yore Len" cause he loves ya and is now going to try something or other else to "cool himself out." Wish I could fuck ya -- that would do it for sure -- sure love.

Well, finally went to dinner -- lunch skipped I think -- I had some soup and crust of roll. The wrestler stayed in cell and told me to "Go ahead, good exercise" (which are my words to him). Actually I'm sure he stayed behind to shit and is too shy to do it in front of others. These people are cynical, shy, screwed, timid, and then aggressive, and the way they talk about women is something else -- no love talk just sex and then they miss their children not their women. The craszy wants to make it with Luci but

she don't dig him. He's here for a year and has a wife and 7 kids but so far no visit or nothing. He told me he's made it with transvestites before (just 2 only -- he made sure to point out), and we had a wild discussion about that, sex in general, specifics of slang and sex and then, of course, horseracing and betting and the lotteries. They read comics and adventure stories and look a lot older than they are.

As I said 99% young guys here so I guess the youth is where the action is; when older, undoubtedly, like everybody else, they slow down or else don't take so many chances or become more sophisticated. Whatever. It's turning out to be a real change of style for me, other than what's happening to me physically, by being here. The more I'm forced into myself the more I realize all the things that are important to me. Mostly I want to get more active and get off my ass, and I don't necessarily mean business or fucking around (except with you) or laying out (cept ditto); but we got to get into something together and build our relationship around a whole bunch of mutual interests or at least be interested in things simultaneously. The money scene will straighten out but time must be used for our own benefit now, and not to collect things (material, knowledge, etc.) but mostly to be alive and to get the cosmic energy flowing through our bodies and minds. That's where it's at and that's where we're going. Bet you never ever thought to see such a long letter but I didn't either under previous circumstances.

There's pigeons outside the window picking at the garbage and it's wild to watch them. So many things to see and at the same time one good thing's enuf if in depth and to the essence. I'm going to your essence ready or not…here I come.

I'm there feeling you now! Remember me, I'm coming home soon soon my sweet beautiful wild and wonderful Annie Apple Annie herself. Think I'll draw again for awhile (just brushed my teeth -- first time since Tuesday -- what a great feeling) and then maybe sleep before I read or work on my "to do" list or writing your again. I'm always thinking of ya --

Flashed on my mother -- hope she's not in the know and all's well with her -- tell her I'll be home soon. Your home, so our home, my home. Our thing is growing as I write. Hope it's so with you too -- love love love len.

———————————

Slept awhile. Time passes so slowly here; it's still light out which means it's before 6 -- wish it was dark already. Maybe tomorrow I go to other building -- I hopahopa.

Had a to-do with the craszy who was jibbing me again. I told him he wasn't acting like a friend to "talk like that" just cause I couldn't under-stand Spanish well (was kidding me about under arm smell). Well, the other two guys came down hard on him and he backtracked and poor kid started to sulk -- I suddenly felt sorry for him. When the wrestler woke up and saw me writing this he asked if I was writing about what happened with the craszy. I said no. ("He's really tuned in, huh.") I told him I was thinking about you, my home and my mother and brother and friends. When you say your mother here it really counts. Wild little children all of these guys and like children mean to one another and then compas-sionate, contrite, etc. Now everybody's trying to cheer up the craszy who's sulking. Some terrific experience, hey! Well, on to Popular Science to see all the things I'm gonna do for you. He's cheered and apologized to me and told me he's my real friend -- I told him to forget it. He's better and so is everybody -- the embarrassed moment has passed. "This too shall pass!!" Finished *Fortune* and clipped out article (tore out I should say), started a book called "Madame" about Helena Rubinstein. Rested a second or two and craszy turned the lights out...talking and writing in the dark. Can't sleep. Music droning nice from the hall (Rock is God in Spanish also). Nobody can sleep except craszy..."came again"...nowhere...2 hours shot...must be 3. Wrestler up and offered me a candy...smoking in dark. I turned on light and only new guy asleep. Now writing and then will read. Thought of reason for no furniture -- could be used as weapons. Guards have only clubs and pipes -- no guns. It's really pleasant here, pen runs in and out of ink, hope it lasts my stay -- asked lawyer for new one tomorrow. Well, I'll try reading. I joking said it's eleven o'clock and the wrestler told me 11:15, said so on radio he said! Doing eye exercises and fasting (almost) -- juice and soup only primarily. It says in book my eyes will get better...it seems so. One good thing anyway other than that is that you're in my heart and mind's eye.

Writing now with my head against toilet and feet upon wall, listening to water hiss - can't stop it, it's like a Chinese torture. Love you -- stay with me, I'm with you. Soon, soon babe...I hope...even sooner than that. Will read now. The boys are all snoring. I'm breathless and exhausted from the books and soon I'll shut the light and try to sleep...I love you the mostest.

━━━━━━━━━━━━━━

My reveille song: morning and sitting in the dark listening to snores, a few crows and the sounds of soon the place waking up! First the guards move furniture in other sections, some toilets flush (I tried to sneak in a quick shit but nothing but hot air), as noise tempo increases the snores get louder and 10 minutes later the banging and keys clanging and voices of men rising in other cells becomes louder and noisier, and someone starts singing. Voices in the hall, keys rattling -- it's reveille for sure! Only a few seconds more and it's here -- it's time to get up. 2 cigarettes and one false shit down, I'm glad I woke up by myself -- will comb my hair and then see if I can brush my teeth before they hustle us out of here. Voice singing like Arab chanter, can't see what I'm writing -- ball point pens aren't good for this, feels like I'm out of ink. It's 15 - 20 minutes now and it looks official -- yep! Here come the guards clanking the keys. Noise will begin in earnest soon. Boys here snoring louder as decibel level and tempo increases -- finished cigarette to filter. Here it comes for real and I'm ready, this will be my day for the move (I hope). Voice singing louder -- I'm still waiting for real wake up to start, metal key banging on metal. Whole place is beginning to stir…snore volume is increasing, wish it would happen already -- "How you gonna keep em down on the farm?" Use bars and clubs and guards, silly! Will put this down and wait for real action to start in a minute or two.

━━━━━━━━━━━━━

Good morning, "I love you, my love, speak with you soon." (Wonder if this is legible.) It's here! Boy, did I get bitten up by my hosts in the mattress, can't get thru jeans though -- good to know. It's really starting now! The day has arrived…doing my exercises…cell still dark. Half hour or so after I got up the whistling, clanging, banging started. Boys still out (one got up and dropped out again in a flash), still dark out although light seeping in…must be 5:30 - 6. Gonna exercise a little more and then check this out…love ya.

━━━━━━━━━━━━━

It's raining people now in corridor. I'm in a lotus position, deep breath-ing (ugh, what air). About 45 minutes later it quieted down although a few more voices out there. Was like the farm awakening and not "Dvorjak Symphony," toilets flushing…noses blowing…it's coming on slow…must be the rain…talking now -- think I'll turn on light and check this out. Looks like my writing got scrambled, and I have to watch those neck-stands or my feet hit toilet when I come down. Foul air…getting stronger in here -- washed up -- real reveille now! Ash cans banging and chief guard is knocking on individual doors. I turned on light and looked out -- "Hello, aqui" -- Everybody's up love. Head count and now we're all talking and I'll finish my exercises and get ready for my walk to mess hall. Good morning love!

They just unlocked the door -- here I go.

"Go know!" -- "Well I'll find out!"

━━━━━━━━━━━

Went to mess hall and saw reflection of sunrise just coming up. Passed by this big good looking cat in suit (first one here) -- mustache and looking like Cesar Romero at his best. He said "Hello Mister" I was too slow to do anything but nod my head and smile, and went on in to eat (sip some coffee). That's the Big Cheese of the place -- tried to say hello or buenos dias to him on way out but you have to keep moving here and his head was turned away so I missed my chance. He sure knew I was American -- that and the way it is here and me (I guess) makes me a celebrity of negative sorts -- hope I stay on the right side of the rating here. Looking forward to the change today -- hope I didn't blow it by not saying "Hello" to Big Man -- but who's to worry -- "Paranoia." Love ya and now back to Helena Rubinstein for a little speed therapy -- love love.

━━━━━━━━━━━

Well, I've been reading and waiting for my lawyer to show up to see about my move, but so far "nada." The book is quick paced, passed description except to say that the woman "Helena" was always on the go -- all business, like an American tycoon (I used to like to think of myself like that), and a weird freak who probably was mostly disgusting but sometimes charming and very very shrewd. Reminds me of the fact that I want less and less to do with business people all the time. But more and more to do with you and love.

I'm anxious to finish this notebook because my paranoia tells me it may get copped or they may take it from me before I get it out. Crazy to fear that but that's how you feel in here -- chasing shadows in your mind. It's about 2 hours now and I just got up and nearly fell down in a "swoon" (get that 20's word!).

Comealongmitmemydear and listen to the "Lullaby of Lennyland." I loveyouthemostest. God, I wish I was with you now. Gonna try to shit again. My body feels good and very bad alternately which considering the circumstances is way out in front. Just wet the pen, it's running out and getting difficult to write with -- was sleeping till craszy turned over and kneed me in the back and I reacted like they jumped me and scared the hell out of us both -- funny, huh!! It's only 8:15. Reveille must be at 5 - 6 or so. Dammit, maybe soon he'll come (lawyer).

One of the girls came by (they own the concessions, make a lot of money, pay off everybody and then buy freedom -- murder $2,000, etc. -- variable fees! Some system but everybody here is the same so it's corruptly democratic in its own way. But I wish I could get out now! Maybe! I hope! They're sweeping the yard, can you imagine that? Well, I'm sure the birds won't starve. Music blasting in hall -- American rock -- sounds good next to snores of my 2 sleeping beauties! New guy reads adventure books and is a nice quiet 25 yr. old car thief (2-10 years!) -- if he can't buy his way out. Occurs to me that's why I'm here, they figure they've got a live one and that I should be hopping to get out at any price. They're right and they know how to wait here cause nothing else is happening except the rip-off and payoff. Let me off and out already!

Must be 10 and I think they're letting us out for exercise. I'll take these notebooks and my book. Hope the lawyer comes with the transfer and the date with the judge set. Well I'm ready. Where is the guy to open the door? Nothing happens here on time.

No, no exercise yet and then my lawyer comes and it's not my lawyer but the American embassy consul rep who said he got a call from N.Y. saying I was being held incommunicado, etc. Gave him details -- said everything stands still here -- no action even tho the fraud complaint had been settled as a misunderstanding. Told him about my heart and gave him Arthur's phone (for his report) and said "Get Me OUT OF HERE." Got his card and gave him my lawyer's card (copied it) and my passport # and he left after 3 - 5 minutes. Looks like a sharp, nice, intelligent guy. Hope he helps get me out quicker -- Good ole Apple and "Ironmountain" themselves!

L awyer still hasn't shown and they came to ask if I wanted a shower. Figured I'd look better for the judge so I said yes. Saw my face in the mirror for the first time since Tuesday last and it's still the same face with a little more grey in the unshaven beard perhaps. This barber chair is the most comfort I've had since Tuesday! So I hope that the Embassy speeds up the act and that there are no more snags. The chiefs here said I'll move today but who knows? Hope my lawyer is seeing Judge now and no problems develop when the Embassy starts inquiring. Don't like the idea of my name being on an Embassy report but I have no 'control' so we'll hope for the best. Anyway, it looks like it'll be soon -- no later than Friday perhaps (who knows) and sooner if I get lucky -- Lucky Lucky Lenny.

The wrestler, craszy and myself are all in here waiting on one other guy to get shaved but I'm comfortable writing in this chair and thankful for the change so I don't give a shit! Drew an ink mark on my sideburns to even them out cause who knows what kind of barber this is. Now I'm gonna take off my shirt so I don't get hair all over but mostly I know it'll turn me on to see my new slender body -- "Nothing like getting off on yourself!" The guy who just got shaved is waiting now for us cause we're all locked in here together and the wrestler is up now and then maybe I'll go or wait for the craszy so I can continue to write. Beside this chair is luxury -- we should have one in our house. Hot now so will take off my shirt and admire! Wait'll you see me -- I can hardly wait to get a hold of you. (Time out for admiration!) Took off shirt and looks great, will take off tee shirt for shave and maybe I'll come mentally at least. I'll always be able to do that -- you know me and "Mirrors! -- "On the wall -- who is -- a donde va! Here I come Leonardo. Dogs barked last nite so tell Duggie I heard her. The shave is without the benefit of cream but I'm looking forward to it. No shower since I've been here. Hope I move today. Wrestler finished, here I go. I would have gotten cut up much worse if I hadn't gotten cream (which I did and the wrestler didn't for some reason -- which is his skin is different from mine and most of the guys' beards are thin). At best though the shave felt like a dull lawnmower and I only came off with a few cuts and stray hairs on my lip which I don't think I'll ask him to fix as he might take off my lip. I just tried it myself and got most of it off with the dull blade. Occurs to me these razors are weapons but this room is inside the gates so the only thing that can happen is you getting killed; but it's doubtful that the guy could get away with it -- some consolation -- but who wants to think about that. That bottom lip of mine is fucked up from that motorcycle accident -- have to get it fixed -- it hurts and I can't stretch it. Right now that should be my biggest problem. I know why it's good here -- I can write with this pen (can't upside down on my back) and there are phlorescent lights in here so I can see. It's so dark in that cell! Well the craszy finished and here we go -- no, not yet. He's gonna get a shave although he's only got a light mustache, some chin whiskers and hardly noticeable (if any) beard after 8 days -- oh well -- he's thru. I love you Len.

═══════════════

Lunch is gonna be soon and I hope that lawyer shows so I know what's happening. Hope good news -- we're ready to go! Back to cell...no lunch yet, lost the young cat -- he went to cell with his brother -- they stole the car together. Wrestler went upstairs maybe to see his brother. Ernie came by and said Todd talked to manager (no lawyer yet). My neck is all red but I'm clean shaven. Starting to feel the cigarettes and should stop but nervousness prohibits. "Where's you self-control, Len?" "What self-control?" Lying down, harder to write on one elbow, such is life and this too shall pass out of here, I hope soon. Will read now and we'll see what happens -- Love Love.

═══════════════

Well, hooray! It's 2 o'clock and the wrestler just told me the guy who just screamed in thru the bars said I'm being transferred at 3 to Todd's building. Either Todd, the Embassy, my lawyer or all of them did it. We exchange addresses, we 3 from 33 and I'm giving the wrestler my mattress, taking my books, etc. and giving the craszy my blanket. Will wash up and get ready for Book III here -- "Qui Vivra Virra" he who lives will see. This is page 36 -- my other football #. Love ya --

We three just smoked 3 cigarettes together (as the Indians, America-nos, I said) and throw the butts into the carton on floor together repeating 1, 2, 3 amigos as we did when we lit them. The 3 from 33! The wrestler said he was sad to see me go but happy for me because it's much better there. I said me also! Santana just played and the craszy called his name -- I thought to myself I'll send them his records and lo and wrestler picked up on my vibes and thoughts as he's done before and said when I get to the States to send them a record. I told him I just thought that myself. He said don't forget and I told him I wouldn't forget my friends (cause they didn't forget me here) and I would remember them all my life as I certainly will. Now, will read again and wait for them to come get me. Never know when here but they said at 3 and that's my number and the next book, Book III, begins on next page (39) which is my age! I'm coming soon babe -- I love you love you love you Apple.

═══════════════

My lawyer came just before 3 and he wanted me to sign a power of attorney but my passport number wasn't right. I'm not sure if that affects my case or not…don't know what to do…so little info…he darted in and darted out. Then Ernie showed me where I was going to live and then we couldn't get out to go back and get my stuff. It was a fuck up for a change but it worked out all right. The lawyer took all the credit for the transfer but I got the news at 2 so it was probably Todd who did it and then the lawyer did it again. He said maybe tomorrow or Thursday but was sure I would get out by Friday. He said he went to court today but couldn't get the judge's decision cause papers did not arrive from Interpol. (Todd asked why he didn't go get them -- I said I didn't know.) Hope he's heavy enuf!!

Also occurs to me that since Arthur didn't pick up my things from the people at Interpol -- who may want (ha) something -- that that's the reason for delay. Have to have you call Bernie (my heart doc.) and send telegram telling about my case: electric shocks, memory loss, fainting spells and observation for heart operation. Hope he doesn't freak out. All in all it's a real hassle with other overtones as well. Don't know what to do -- if I'll get out immediately or be held up. I'm

sweatin' like hell. Anyway this part of the place is a palace -- I'm still on the floor but the guys here are really organized. Do their own cooking, sell you anything, make phone calls for you, etc. They're mostly older and all real sharp. A heavy mixture from murderers to smugglers, et al.

I'm gonna sleep on floor, no bed available in room but sure glad I'm here. Sitting, waiting to take a shower -- thank goodness! Played some chess and dominos before and Todd came in to say goodnite -- after a head count up against wall. The hardest thing here until you venture near guards and then it changes. People have tried to escape and I've heard all sorts of stories from Nat'l Guard in here and everybody in yard naked and beaten with flat side of a heavy machete to electrodes on balls, etc. Enuf to scare the shit out of you, and if a person gets sentenced they go

to Devil's Island (Wow). Anyhow I'm still writing and reading and trying to learn Spanish by talking and probably making great headway under the circumstances. I'm still on diet-fast and don't know what I'll do about that -- I'll make the decision after Friday. Things are going to finalize soon and I'm trying to keep myself together as well as I can.

I miss you the moistest and I wish we didn't have to go thru this but life is full of surprises and you have to take it as it falls. People have gone thru worse, but I sure don't feature it.

Wish I could tell you all the beautiful things I think of you but I'm too nervous to write now so I'll kiss you a million times and wish you the bestest -- of Love and Longing and Fulfilment. I hope I make it but if I don't you know I Love You forever and ever and ever and ever and alla time Love Lenny.

Just took a shower, shampoo, anti-perspirant and powder and do I feel great! Not as good as the Baths with my amigo A.D. but still great! These guys are all heavy -- average age 42 or so; one old guy in his 60's -- all very executive looking, very nice and they try to make you feel relaxed…it's a lot lot better. There's 12 people in this cell with one head guy. Hope you is being good. I luvs ya a lot -- Lucky Lenny.

Well, it's morning and I feel like I'm 45 years old -- whatever that means. Slept on the floor on a mattress last night and couldn't go to sleep for hours. Finally fell out after 4 cigarettes and 2 hours, was hot and cold. Heard reveille in other cell blocks, it's about 30 yards away and then the mess hall banging! Everybody here slept on till head count, about 1-1/2 hrs later and then went back to sleep. Since I'm sleeping on space where dining table is we folded my mattress then went out into corridor (about 30 yds long) and took some exercise walking up and down and bought some hot chocolate (thru the bars at the end of corridor is a concession). Got one of the wildest spit shines ever in hall for 1 Bs. Next I brush my teeth and shave myself (they've got everything here). It's 8:30 now. Funny how great shaving is just for something to do. The ice man came for the cell commissary and they chopped it up and are dressing chickens (steak also) for the day. I'm saving taking a shower for later and then another at nite. Todd came in (he's going to Court -- doesn't know if they'll take him), wonder if that could drag

my stay out?? Probably could!!! Finishing Rubinstein book then will start on something else, tho I ran out of reading material. They have a laundry service here and was putting on my brown pants but took them out in case I go to see Judge. I hope sooner but think probably Thursday. Am writing smaller now as I'm running out of paper (1 more page left) and I don't want that to happen or I'll flip out! The head of cell gave me his shaving stuff, etc. and I offered him 5 Bs. which he refused. That's unusual here cause everybody is on the take, just shows you where these guys are at -- all big-timers. They do crossword puzzles, chess, etc. -- the executive branch of crime here, so as an 'Executive of whatever' it's much better here. Boy, I'm sweating like mad. Having a phone call made this morning to Arthur to come Wednesday so I can find out what's happening and tell him what's in my head. I sure haven't been kept informed and I'm shaky about the lawyer. Have no place to lie down so am sitting on someone else's bed, don't want to lie on it. Will go lie on Ernie's if he went to court. I've got my

brown pants and sport shirt folded and ready to jump into for court if I go -- although I'm wary of looking too good or too bad cause they could hit me up for more or let me languish -- paranoia again! They're sweeping the floor again, place is spotless and I'm gonna stop writing now.

I wonder what you're thinking and if you still love and believe in me. It's hell not being able to call you (or anyone for that matter), but worse not to hear you or touch you or everything else that's you and me together. I believe I'll get out Friday cause that's what the Feds here said when they brought me and since they've got the papers which the Judge is waiting for I guess and hope they know and don't hold me on some other technical charge. So anyway, here I am and there you are and no telephone or anything -- if I could just hear your voice.

Haven't exercised today cause I have no room to do it, but I'll figure out somewhere to do it later. Hope and pray you're still with me and that my mother's not in the know or worried. Hope and hope and hope so much about everything. It's almost like I'm at a play -- as an audience participant -- cause everything seems so unreal here in relation to me. Soon I hope to be able to laugh and joke about my vacation experience here, but for now it's "Unreal -- Unreal" as M.G. would say. I love you so much I can't stand it, I guess the exceptions do prove the rule cause being away from you has driven me crazy. Boy do I look forward to you. Be true. I love you. Send my heart to the kids and animals and do yourself up for me for now. I'll be there soon soon. My Love Len.

Well, I'm out in the exercise yard and ball players (punch ball) active -- it's a courtyard surrounded by 5 tiers of cells. Crazy way to play ball cause the people who are in cells above are not privileged to come down here so they're mad and throw things. I got hit twice with a piece of bread and something else before I caught wise and got under the eves of the building where there's no sun but protection. Played some chess with a cell mate and bang someone threw a big crock of something down 10 yds away, which crashed and broke (could have broken someone's head). Cans, bottles, water come down and they look at it and keep playing! Won 1 out of 4 games in chess and spoke to a few murderers, robbers, etc. The law here is weird as they can hold you here for 3 months even if innocent. I have to get American consul here again and try to pressure the authorities: talked to a Panamanian and it seems the 7 day number has to do with the law here -- if they keep you 8 days without going before a judge they have to let you go. So it'll be Thursday for the judge and I hope all goes well. I told Arthur to come tomorrow so I can find out what's happening -- the lawyer tells me zip. His assistant came and I signed the power of attorney (hope it doesn't fuck me up).

Was in next cell most of the day bullshitting in Spanish then in English with Todd. He's looking at 12 years (6 with good behavior) for his number. Get a Spanish dictionary and books and did a Spanish-English number here with Ernie. I spoke Spanish and he spoke in English or tried to. And, oh yes I was robbed (funny) when I went to the mess hall for juice. Some guy picked my pocket (a pen); I felt it, turned around and saw who it was (a trustee) but didn't hassle it. I had borrowed the pen and when I told the guy what happened he said, "Is that all he took?" I said yes, and he said "Ha, you're lucky." Guess I am. Then came into my cell (they lock you up at 6) and bullshitted with a cat who speaks pretty good English. He shot and killed his girl -- a sensational case here -- they caught him in Columbia. Everybody here is groovy to me. I thought they were in their 40's but the oldest is 32 except for one old guy (here for hitting someone with a chair in a fight and breaking his arm -- 15 days). The other cats are murderers (5 here) and fraud cases of bum checks up to $250,000. Cell quite sophisticated and maximum term they get, if they have money is 1 - 3 years.

Was really fucked up today as time passed very slowly, every hour feels like five. Think about you oh so much and wonder how you're taking this and if you're still "my Bebe" -- "You better be." I've lost so much weight my tight jeans slip off my hips to ankles without opening them -- lost 3" off waist, maybe. I'm gonna continue writing and reading by candle, it's 10 only but they're all getting ready for bed cause tomorrow is visitor's day starting at 8:30 and everybody's very excited. So am I and I only hope Arthur shows. I asked about 3 people to call him including lawyer's assistant but I also asked him to have the lawyer show today and he never did, so who knows where reliability is. The guy here who said he'd have his brother call apparently didn't reach Arthur cause the brother wrote down the wrong #. Gave message to a policeman or vigilanti or whatever -- a really smooth cat and nice -- he tired right away but no one home so he said he'd call again later for me but who knows -- we'll see?

Gonna take shower now as they're getting ready to fall out and all mattresses are down except mine -- More soon.

Took shower, mattress down but we bullshitted for 3 hours about N.Y., Cuba, women, sex, cars, drugs, love and Cuba (sex) -- catch the dialogue later you'll dig it! Lo and behold a bed came in and one of the guys (he's got 4 bullet holes in him, fought in the revolution here, and his father is a general, etc.) insisted I have it for tonite. So I slept pretty good (5 hours) -- one of the guys shot up and wanted to know if I wanted some,

I declined. They said 75 % pure -- Wow! Norbo! Finally fell out at 1 after we were firmly entrenched in an all topics heated (animated) discussion. They jibe each other continuously like little boys -- goosing each other, kidding, etc. -- it's amazing, such sophisticated babes! Went to sleep; was gonna jerk off but fell out before I could touch myself. I love ya and send you sweet hellos.

─────────────────

I t's morning and the guard came in who was gonna make the call for me, said no one was home last nite. So that leaves the lawyer's assistant to have reached him. The guard will call again this morning and I'm sure he's been contacted -- (ha!) Was funny the guard sitting on my bed looking at my books and pad. Asked if I was writing a diary and I said No, only imaginary -- don't want any vibes about what's in here! But he saw me writing and I knew he would cause I didn't start till after he was seated. I thought he had noticed before and would be suspicious if I tried to hide anything. No matter he's cool, I hope. It's visitor's day and no mattresses on floor, extra mattresses doubled up on beds. "Be nice everybody." So to finish for now, I've got a towel around my head, Arab style, and I'm look-ing forward to Arthur to get the news and give him a whole list of things for my defense -- (I've been writing and analyzing). Cell number will be called out soon so I wanna finish, put my stuff away and review my notes for Arthur, who'll hopefully get here at 8:30. Hope I can get Dr. Olementi down here today to examine me in order to present a medical certificate at court tomorrow as to my present "bad" condition.

My jeans keep falling off -- the stitching on the belt came out so the pants are separating from the belt line. No belt -- gave it to Arthur so they won't cop it. Hope he got my camera he said they (a secretary at Inter-pol) called him but he wouldn't see her as he doesn't like blackmail! (and I'm sitting here). That may be the reason why my papers aren't here from

Interpol -- they might want some loot! I'm gonna lay it on him today if he comes. Lawyer told me Judge only Tues. or Thurs. but he turns out to be full of shit again as it's every day. Really builds confidence and acute stomach and paranoia pains. Paranoia appears a lot in these pages but I've sure got it and everything I see and hear here more than justifies it. So I'm saving my good pants for tomorrow for the judge if that lawyer doesn't fuck up and maybe I'll be out Friday (I hope, I hope). Oh, Apple how I miss you. (Tears just came to my eyes and I'm writing all choked up now and I want you to know I think about you all the time. Hope you're still hanging in there.)

━━━━━━━━━

They just gave me a fried cheese thing, I took 3 bites to be polite and am looking to throw it out the window. I did. Nobody believes I had a heart attack (think it's a ploy; somehow it seems more real to me here cause it's a lot like a charity hospital ward with bars and guards) -- and also I look younger than these guys who actually I'm 5 - 10 years older than. Second in age to the old man. Proves my theory about the young in action, etc. I'm opening up a little to these guys here but it's okay. ("Shaft" music just started on radio) We just turned on the lights and soon floor'll be swept to pretty up for visitors. "Numero" is soon. That's Reveille! File out in hall and then maybe I can get my hot chocolate. One or two faces in here I never remember -- they're faceless. One a guy about 50 -- so I'm the third (3 again, yeh) oldest. Just noticed him again -- in and out of vision but doesn't talk. The other is a cop who killed somebody when off duty -- he's never around or I just don't register him. Oh those 3 bites just fucked up my stomach, was like a deep fried something or other stuffed with a matzorella type cheese. It's the 30th (another 3). Had my heart attack on the 30th also, so I guess it's gonna be a heavy day. Well here goes! I love ya a lot and more than the pen can describe. I'm coming home soon. Love Len.

What a day! Visitors came in hordes...people all over. Ernie's wife left him (his wife left him -- ha, other way around kiddo). People introduced me all around, met his brother who is assistant manager of Hilton. Free weekend, maybe! Made some political contacts, etc. -- it was a zoo and exhausting. Finally Arthur came (Good Ol' Arthur) and brought me news and pads to write on. Gave him my list and analysis of situation as it now stands.

I'll be out Friday cause they can only keep you 7 days and on the 8th day they have to charge you or let you go. So it's all a money game or to fuck up that wise-ass American who didn't know nothing! Right now I'm feeling good. Didn't know that I hadn't been charged yet. Just under investigation and a Judge has to make the decision whether to make a charge or not. Heard that from Todd's conversation with Arthur (he hadn't clued me until then either), so I guess that's what it is. Arthur says it has to go to 2 Judges which means I might get charged and then the case heard (my interpretation and I hope it's paranoia) but I'll ask lawyer tomorrow or find out myself after I see Judge, if I see him.

Anyhow, was feeling great until I just analyzed it this much further, which means if lawyer didn't get all the stuff ready he won't go to the Judge or else he'll have to because of 7 day rule and Judge won't be able to rule till all info is in (or will have to charge me in order to keep me here) and then when info is in 2nd Judge would hear it and then act on case. Which means I'll have an official arrest and I'll be here a while, probably 1 - 2 weeks more and it'll cost more money cause they now gotta reason for it. Hope all the info is together so Judge can act! Anyhow, we'll see -- boy did I take this far out. That's how it is down here. (I just lay down to write and it feels soo good!) Anyhow just undid myself again -- shows you how it can change.

But if a person is really together they can take whatever comes and deal with it the best they can (not sure I did so good but I did-did anyhow). If a person's soul is in the right place it's all okay cause this is unfortunately what's happening now and I have to adjust to it and be together or I'll get fucked and then I'd be nowhere for myself and you or anybody. What good does that do if I can't change anything or do other than I'm doing! If you as my love help me to help me elevate myself and vise versa then that's the trip -- the one you lay on yourself.

Arthur brought me my pills and can get 2 doctor's certificates with a little bread. Lawyer is connected and should know (negligence lawyers do -- so should be or else he's weak.) It'll cost some more money though and that's the game here between cops, lawyer and Judge. Just went to see Todd but he's in the shower doing a joint up. (There's lots of good grass in this section, and cocaine.) Hope my passport cleared by now. But anyhow enuf of this trauma. I did myself up in the shower and am flying high -- bout time cause couldn't handle it anymore. So back to where I'm at: is whatever happens I'm hanging in there best I can. I'll live through it I hope, so time will tell (what shades of Marty Green). Nothing but nothing is gonna stand in our way even if they kill me cause it's US is happening now and it'll always be -- cause now is always. If I could have doped this out and not have to have gone through this soul searching.

Arthur told me you called and said you "Loved me," but I know how he talks so you're probably more than a little fucked up...hope you're getting my vibes and being okay. I cried a little while talking about you and the rush of emotion nearly wiped me out, so I'm gonna just take it as it comes and deal with it that way. Doing my best to be consistent with my interests and keep everybody else involved with me covered and I hope same is happening on all other sides too including the lawyer who may be playing the nice guy game or not, we'll soon know. In any case I don't see it going past 2 more weeks so I'm ready and whatever happens will happen with me smiling. I Love Ya so much -- get ready I'm coming soon!

═══════════

Came back to room and got into a wild discussion about politics, philosophy, astro projection, Einstein and atoms, matter and non-matter with one of the murderers and after it was over I smiled but he and everybody were a little overpowered and I think it's okay though. Then did same with Todd on a personal basis, I bullshitted up a storm about me, him and Life. He's only 21 but very groovy with a lot of gaps yet but a good guy and nice friend. Musicians and dropouts and groovys really get to me. Then did a joint (in the shower again) and now I'm finished writing. Must rest cause I'm exhausted -- Love ya the moistest always always Leonardo. That is my name down here -- funny, huh! I see you and all the ones I love in spots in the air and my mind's eye alla time. Stay with me, I'm with you and you know it -- hooks in your heart babe.

═══════════

Just saw Todd and he said 2 doctors are necessary to get you to a hospital. I figure he (lawyer) wants 2 doctors to cover my testimony and that Interpol is charging me with lying -- no longer anything to do with fraud complaint. We'll see -- Todd agrees but he says 1 week at the most. I say FRIDAY, but I'm with you forever.

Just had some soup and that is all and I'm writing on my back Again... speak to ya later -- love Len.

═══════════

I'm exhausted and gonna try to sleep soon -- been reading and started to get really hungry. All my body's coming down but my soul's going up, I love ya. Just showed my Yoga book to General Boy and he's going at it and asking me some questions -- Funny! Well I'm On -- 2nd time today. Tell you about it later and it's fine -- real fine. I love ya. Well tomorrow always will come and never does so 'in this moment.' I tell you -- only you, only me -- together. Don't forget me -- I'm coming -- ah at last -- Len the Axe.

Thursday. Oh the sleep of exhaustion. Slept like a dead man and woke up just before they (guards) screamed "Numero." Fortunately everybody else was even more bushed and the head of cell winked at one of the guards and they counted us in the room. There's 13 of us and everybody but me went back to sleep (except for 3 others -- 2 who work here and one older man). I got up, took a shave and a ohh-cold shower (although it's luke-cold in the morning as they attempt to give you hot water then). Oh you'd love it -- keeps you moving -- shades of Peru. So now I'm writing and next I'll walk in hall and read and wait for my appearance in front of the Judge. I don't say a word. It seems only the lawyer is allowed to talk and you just stand there (I'm told handcuffed although if I'm not charged, will I be?). Got my good duds -- the pants (brown Venezuelan) and shirt (airplane) ready to jump into and I'm gonna try to not smoke so many cigarettes today as I'm starting to feel em -- 1 pack only, hear! Hope everybody is doing okay with all my problems! My mother probably doesn't know -- although she usually knows when something is wrong.

Well, Boy Scout Camp here is crazy and I'm probably the coolest today since I've been here, and since I analyzed my case last nite. Wonder how I'll be after the Judge -- we'll see. Gonna study Spanish all day today and write and then try to do some exercise. I hope my partner on the outside is doping out the situation here and I wish he'd send me some info. That's the thing that bothers me most -- not knowing what the score is. Wonder how I'm doing in my other business affairs? Hope good as we're gonna be here in good shape yet -- especially after all these dues, I'm more determined than ever. But I'm really determined mostly to find a good and rich new life for us in everything, but mostly to be together and work and live and smile) ah yes it's sometimes hard to smile but that's the clue otherwise you do yourself in), and be together forever. God, how I miss you. Love sure gives you an energy rush -- sometimes up and sometimes bad but for sure a rush nonetheless. I'm sitting here on one of the cat's beds with the towel wrapped around my head and a blanket around my shoulders. Look like an Arab-Cherokee Indian -- which ain't so bad for these parts. Gonna put away my mattress and take my walk and get a hot chocolate -- will pick up later -- Love you all. May this day smile on us -- forever yours, Len.

Took the walk, hot today -- then studied some Spanish and English with Ernie and sat around and played at picking at a guitar. We then all had to go down to the patio and the circus there was incredible! Had a few conversations with some killers and robbers, read, and outlined my new Yoga program and tried to sit in the sun; but it's too dangerous with the stuff crashing into the courtyard and a slap-ball game and a soccer game going on at the same time in the same space. People sitting at the ends of the patio continuously ducking the flying balls, but somehow everybody makes it. My lawyer's not here yet and I don't know whether I've been charged or not so if I haven't been I'll get out mandatorily tomorrow. If I have been without my knowing it (as could be), it'll drag out for 1 - 2 weeks probably as outer limit; unless they're really out to fuck me up for some reason having to do with my testimony which they made me sign without a lawyer or anybody and it was in Spanish! So I really don't know. I wish my partner would send me a written explanation of everything that is and has happened -- just so I don't have to go thru all these question continuously in my head. Came back upstairs had some juice and fruit cocktail and bullshitted about Yoga which is enabling me to do it here myself. I'll do a complete session today by turning the other guys here on to it. Gonna read "Future Shock" today but am trying to finish my writing for now so I can get all my thoughts down and be able to ask the lawyer all the questions in my mind and hope he can explain it to me in English. I'm gonna try to get Todd upstairs so he can translate and read the guy for me and see if he can better tell me where he's at.

I'm just worn out waiting and wondering what's up...with no one to discuss it with. I'm sure my friends are trying everything they can to speed up this process but I don't know if they have all the information. So I'm about finished for now and this book will remain incomplete if the lawyer comes as it has my questions in the back for Arthur, et al. Gonna get off again today and that should help but that has its own paranoia -- but I believe it's cool but if I don't do something it just intensifies the tension. So anyhow the waiting is the worst and I hope it won't be long because things in New York must be getting very weird for me with reference to a few of my numbers there. Hope I hope soon -- but if not there's nothing more that I can do except writing and questioning and hope that helps. So time, which resolves all questions even with a non-answer will tell its story soon. Can only be a lifetime and I'm determined not to blow my cool, but I sure wish I knew more as the doubts are what bug you. I love ya in a million different ways and wish I was with you. Oh so sweet you are and now I know what love is in the deepest pits of my soul and I'm ready to act on it and let it all flow thru. I Love You! Later and soon my love -- 36 was my college football number and today's the 30th a (3) so here's good luck to us babe -- Axe.

Just woke up; slept about 2 hours -- someone copped this pen and I just got it back. No lawyer -- no judge; if nothing today and not charged I'll be out tomorrow -- that's what they said when they brought me over -- if charged I'll be here a while. What a thing not to know how long! The only thing to say is that the guys here are all in the same boat, only some are here years before brought to trial. They did something, most of them, but for the most part it's strictly money and waiting waiting waiting to find out when do I get out.

My heart attack -- and my life is sure changed. Everybody now is tuned in to me and feeding me soup whenever I'll take it. Todd says I'm really getting thru to these guys and I figure although I didn't come on to them (they did to me -- mostly to learn Yoga) that the more friends I have here the better the insurance. They sure get a kick looking out for the big strong nice Americano and that's just fine with me! Still no lawyer and I now find out it's 8 days here -- then release; but it's the weekend so it's impossible to get out before Monday, so I've resigned to myself to whatever happens. Nothing I can do anyhow but either give myself the best trip I can here (which I'm trying to do --I'm even starting to laugh a little) or put myself on a bummer which won't do me or anybody else any good…so I'm hanging in. Wish I could see you and my family (everybody) but the thought of you carries me to a lot of beautiful places. All we've had…some thoughtful…some terrible moments to contend with since we've met but the good's just arriving…I can feel it. It's so weird what being here does to you. I think now I could almost become a "taster of life to its utmost sensitivities" cause for the second time in a little over a year I've been brought back to the reality of what I have going for me to make me happy…what things yet to feel…what high moments to tread through this crazy labyrinth called time and Love Love Love you babe fantastic woman! You're my conduit thru to bliss…I'm a comin' don't worry and when I see you it'll be better than ever. Luvs ya the best somehow now than ever before, but it's oh so sweet and times' marches are gonna bring US to new highs in everything we do and Are You Ready AppleAxe!!

Fucking place is full of surprises. Had a visitor; thought it was lawyer but it was the red headed detective from Interpol (who gave me his couch to sleep on) who came to say hello! He said he has my camera and bag and what did I want to do with it. I asked him to bring it to my attorney. He refused bread for it and said he'd bring it over to him tomorrow and not to worry. He appears to come from a good family here and isn't looking for anything, just a friend (I hope and believe). We'll see if he drops it off. Anyway gave me his office and home # (don't think he's spying cause he's groovy handsome cat). We speak French together and he said not to worry but if I needed him or anything to call and he'd come and was very nice. That's like a fantastic sort here -- I believe him! I came back to room and the General's nephew, Pedro, who's related to head of customs (all uncles) came on to me friendly as a friend and said anything that's his is mine -- especially if I needed contacts (Public Relations he called them -- funny) and outlined several groovy numbers. Everyone is like taking me on and it's getting better. The chief of the room (a real 36 year old smoothie -- $250,000 check #) just laid some tension relaxer on me 00 get you there he said! Everybody being groovy and I can use all the friends I can get here. After I get out I'll see what happens, but as of right now I'm a lot cooler and getting ready (if I'm not already) for whatever happens. I think the worst is I won't get out till end of next week -- maybe sooner, I hope...later babe...Len.

Been reading and my boy here just shared his locker with me (my other pair of pants and shirt, good ones, have been in a bag on the top of locker with my books) and said again anything of his is mine. These guys are wild, when they like you they go all out and he likes me which is nice cause he's here for murder but will be out because of family and $2,000 (which is nothing) in a month when he goes to a hospital and then goes home 2 weeks later -- some #! But I'm open to an extent with them and they dig me so it's comfortable here -- I mean compared only to where I was -- this is the "Palace."

I'm running down the case in my mind for tomorrow when I hope the lawyer will come (I asked the detective Miguel to ask him to) or we see the judge or whatever. The domino game just broke up and maybe I'll get into bed and read and go to sleep early cause I'm really exhausted again. It's mental I guess but otherwise I guess I've sort of adjusted to the situation for now until something new turns up. I just took the relaxing medicine the cat gave me and I should be able to sleep good, good nite My Love, Len (only 1 pack of cigarettes today).

Slept like a log for 3 - 4 hours and then intermittently. Got up before "numero" and was about to shower when they called it so had to get all dressed to go out into the hall. The Big Shots (2 - 3 of them) just sleep on. Took a shower, shave and squeegied off floor and now sitting at table with towel around my head writing; put on my new pants for Good Luck (to get out today) but somehow not too hopeful. I think the 2 Drs. certificates, etc. just weren't gotten yet, although if I'm not charged (I'll ask lawyer or Arthur when they come) I'll be out after weekend.

Weird pimple in middle of scar on my arm which I squeezed and that provided 5 minutes of entertainment. Gonna go study Spanish with Ernie and then read "Future Shock" (a soberly approach to what's happening in our culture -- the info is good but the language is very textbook). Just smoking the last cigarette in pack from yesterday and today I'm going to cut it out for the day -- maybe -- but that depends on what and how I feel today. Right now feel good physically (no pain), got my pills in my pocket (not too paranoid), and about to go walk in hall -- then Spanish -- then read and as usual bullshit with the guys.

Got new underwear and socks as a present from General's nephew and feeling clean except for the sweaty tee shirt I'm wearing. Thank goodness I got my pocket dictionary. I'm not able to attempt all the Spanish newspapers. Went to visit the wrestler with one of the Big Guys (5'6" & a murderer) from my room and he said the craszy was really glad to see me. I suddenly found I couldn't talk and I told them I'd be back on the morrow. Good Kats and I feel for them when I saw them in that cell 33 with 2 other new guys; but they were really smiling and oh so proud that their clean-cut Americano (me?) came to visit. Gonna give them 10 Bs. to help them out. Wow, what an emotional rush I just had, so I'm gonna go out now and do my things in hall, etc. and wait to see if lawyer comes, and check my name on list for judge (don't believe it's there but alas "who knows here!").

I Love Ya…need ya…and think constantly of that apple dance and face and all the beautiful things we have together…Later my love, Len the Axe.

━━━━━━━━━━━━━━━━━━━━━━━━━━━━━━━

Took my walk, had a hot chocolate and suddenly spied "Future Shock" on a table in Spanish and started talking with these young cats. They seem to be really trying and I discussed that and Einstein's book, etc.; told them I wanted to show the book to my friend (in Spanish) and gonna go get it later -- nice cats. Now sitting in a canvas back chair with my feet up on a stool writing. Somebody copped my Yoga Book and Pedro is fuming mad and I had to tell him to take it easy, it's a weird possession trip! Jimmy just came on the radio "I'm Losing You" reminded me of Devin -- wow! "Jesus but I've got things to do when I get out of here!" Got my Spanish book ready, just bought a cartoon book, have another pad "to do" on one side and Spanish vocab words to look up on the other, "Future Shock" to read and this pad to write in. Maybe my Yoga book is in Todd's room, but this morning I did my full half-hour plus. Pedro now hanging up my clothes (he sent for a hanger and put my other stuff, empty pads, socks (1) and articles I cut out in a new bag for me. He's really cool and straight -- just awfully nice. Gives everybody some of his food of which he gets ample supply and is always smiling and talking, nice guy, has 3 - 4 bullet holes in him; killed a guy (bang) and a really nice guy nonetheless. I'm really tired and weary and wish I could just get outside into the sun and air. Boy do I miss it, and you and a million things one doesn't miss until you can't get to them. The world's really changing and I've been living too much within myself and the past (as an excuse) for non-living, but that's over and in that sense this experience is giving me a shot of energy which is going to take us a long way. "No more Tristesse (Sadness) -- it's our turn to tune into the Happy -- Our trip as we make it and Make it Happy We Will!" Boy what determination!

Music is wild, dancing, running around the globe -- sex, love, you, me, everything Here we come. Believe me I'm turning this # into a good one and gonna get the best out of it, as we should do with everything that comes our way because events are just interpreted by ourselves as Good or Bad. "Make the best of it" means literally make it the best way you can for the events as they come down. We can't control 'em anyhow so that's the only thing to do. Boy, I'm smiling and it sure feels good. Think I'll take a bite of the Apple… Um Um Good! And there better be plenty more cause I'm coming home soon Babe with all this energy and my body's gonna get straight cause I'm taking care of it now real good and I'm gonna take care of you and all and everything I love. We're gonna have a really beautiful Life Trip; the one that somehow all this shit we go thru either gets you ready for or not. La Dolce Vita -- Oh the Sweet Sweet Life! I'm finally ready and Now even here I'm tuning into what's happening to me this minute -- even tho it's what it is! I can feel its effects. People are grooving on me and I'm starting to groove on this hell hole of a Boy Scout Camp. Now music is blaring and I just started to dance to "It's Too Late Baby" (Ha), and everybody got turned on and all is smiles and Happy. I'm writing this and dancing at the same time! Enuf now for my Spanish and I'm gonna whistle and sing and dance and do it up all day. I just turned up the music -- blast -- and everybody's dancing, singing, etc. It's happening, I'm into it and I'm coming home soon. Full of the right juice for a change. Here we go. Let's get into it…it's all our own Trip as we make it. Life is what you want it to be whatever you do or wherever you find yourself, only you can interpret it to the Up or Down or Good and Bad. So I'm into it Now and I'll be coming Home Soon My beautiful Love Cat; and then all the shit you're going thru now will seem like the counter-base for the Happy that we're into together. It's gonna get Better and Better and Better alla time. We're gonna be here and it's gonna work -- you'll see, but no matter where it is, it (Life) is gonna work for US instead of US for it. Boy, Pedro is sweeping and cleaning the whole place like crazy, won't let anybody help because it's one of the few constructive things you can do here and who wants to give that up. Creativity! Yes we have to create and interact to turn on ourselves…Body, Mind, Soul and exposure to the Earth Elements. Saying this from in here is like "contemplating your navel," but I feel it. It's right on and I know now I'm gonna be happy (whatever that is) for all my Life, come what may and come with You. It's all gonna be not all-right but all-there and wow are we in for a trip -- it's just a question of attitude and how you view it is how you see it and how you feel it. It's far out, Life and I'm gonna take the Bite out of the "Apple of Life" -- "Join me, it's Our Trip" -- You're the one I need So let's Go -- Don't Delay -- Come Mit Me, I'm Comin Home Baby --I Luvs Ya Apple -- The Axe Man Lenny.

Friday. Well it's working, things all coming my way. The chief of room just laid some tea on me and Pedro gave me a pair of gum-sealed knit-top shoes "A souvenier de Venezuela" he said. I'm writing Spanish now and waiting again. It's 9:25 AM and I'm feelin good…good babe.

It's now 11:20, read a little Spanish then Carlo (boxer and lover) showed me word root ending of Spanish (he's the one I talked about Einstein with) and then he sewed up my shoes for me so they'd stay on. Now Pedro doing the other one and soon Candy for the NOSE and up up and away as they say -- can hardly wait and where's that lawyer and what's happening -- cause there's a chance I could get out today but "qui sais!"

I hand wrestled the heavy here and beat him in one/half second with a smile and then took a most satisfying shit. I ate an egg this morning and you know what eating can do to your system! Well anyway where's my lawyer with the good news? I wish my partner was here so we could discuss the pros and cons and mostly so I'd know what's happening. I'm sure he does. Oh well I'm hoping it's getting done fast (which is my only doubt) cause I know I'll be out soon, I'd just like it to be Now! Todd came in; saw his father and he's got a good shot at the hospital #, (1 month there and out), hope he makes it! Then went to bathroom and Pedro was shitting and we did a joint up and now back at bed. Guy from next room who looks like Barry with a Vandyke came in -- he's gonna fast for 3 days starting this morning and gave him some info on hot water and lemon. A really good smiling-eyed cat. Aldo (chief) sat down -- calls him his brother and me too. Todd had a fight with Aldo and he's across the room talking with Carlo, who did my shoes (armed robbery -- bit #) funny parallel scene.

Took walk in hall with Todd and concessionère did us up with supply of joints, it should be nice plus hot today included. Came back into room again and Big Murderer did me up with some nose-candy and I'm frozen into the beauty of all cats tuned in on me and me getting off on it and the things as well as the vibes. It's really happening…coming my way…feel good.

No lawyer. Shirt went to laundry and won't be back till morrow. If I get out I'll give it to Pedro. So here I am gonna Future Shock myself back to myself. Later love and soon oh so soon and oh so fine. A Big Huge Taste of Fine and Happy and Love and ALL of US -- ALLAUS!!

3 9…all alone…disoriented from initial achievement drives, ups downs not important now but shaped NOW. Now is what's happening and should shape now to future nows so to live in accordance with the Energy Flow and not try to reverse process (to get back what's gone and live in the past). Now and Future Nows is the Direction and the Goal is Happy. With it physically, mentally (cool head), and spiritually (the 3 astro planes), where we came from and where we are going.

Well gave a Yoga class then sang some songs with Todd and then came in and sat down to read. Did a joint courtesy of the chief and then into my mind came the thread of imaginary things which surpassed the writing as I now see everything come into place.

No lawyer yet but he could come and get me out cause they let you out at 5 - 6 p.m. so we'll see but not too hopeful, too bad. But this is Friday, 3:30 (still time), and would have felt worse 2 days ago if not out by Now! Good thing I'm living in the NOW. Well it's 5:30 and lawyer didn't show. I wish I knew what was going on; well I'll get a call out to Arthur and he should fill me in on Sunday when he comes. Only this time I'm writing a long list of questions and I want answers. Anyhow it's like okay here except the strain and vibes from everybody else makes it crazy even if you're cool. But settling down now for some rest in the evening. "Future Shock" is such a bore to read, a research document, cause of the way it's written it's a bore with the message obscured by the pedantic structural research annotated, etc. pieced together conclusion. No Free Flow. A research project. But it's right on in its descriptions of what's happening but to say it 20 - 200 different ways is bullshit and ob- scures the major point of the book. But maybe that's all the cat has to say. If he can only be a reporter and play that tune time and time again. He's missing the mass audience that he wants to reach (maybe). The people he's trying to prepare for Life, Bullshit, etc. I think the book's okay but I wish I read faster so I can get thru it cause I want to get to where I learn something new. I'm sure it's there on the last page and maybe I should read that first.

===

Well here I am and that's that so I'm gonna study a little ole Spanish and see what else is doing next door cause that's about it. Shit, I thought there was a chance to get out today but it looks like next week. At least by then I hope to know the score. I'll bet they're trying to hang a perjury testimony rap on me for the fun of it, and money, and laying a bad trip on an Americano. So here I am and here I go -- Smile! I love ya. Been a little crazy (a lot) the whole nite…it seems to go on forever. Have to read on "Meditation" tomorrow -- but lawyer didn't come, didn't see judge -- nothing and started to feel closed in. John Wayne in "True Grit" was shown in Dining Room -- (mess hall whadayamean D.R.) and it was unbelievable bad, and gave me a headache. I came back, did a joint and just took some medicine so maybe I'll sleep as soon as they take the table off my floor and so good nite my Love. I'm thinkin' on ya. Pray for me I Loves ya. Me -- Len the Axe -- AppleAxe.

===

Well woke up this morning "numero" and then slept another 2 hours (it was best sleep I've had). Got up, did my Yoga (45 mins) then showered (no shave, fuck it) and walked the hall. Got a hot chocolate, but not eating solids (although had a chocolate bar for some quick energy -- boy do you get sluggish here -- never realized how much getting outside means till your inside). Couldn't read so I walked up and down hall and then did a little more exercise.

The lawyer came -- hooray! Said I haven't been charged -- 8 days Interpol and 8 days in front of judge -- maximum 16 days if not charged. So

Tuesday is 14 days and Thursday is 16. That's when he says I get out (and I doped it out technically the same altho these guys here say only 8 days -- then free -- then they could arrest you right away again). The lawyer said I'd be free but I can't leave country until investigation is closed. It doesn't matter that claimant withdrew charge; they can pursue it on their own because claim was made (that's info from in here). I in turn can have the other guy arrested (but no eyes for that although these guys talk of other alternatives -- Ha). Sitting on beach chair with feet on stool muy comfortable. Then until investigation is completed I can be picked up again and can't leave country but that should take another week. If it drags out after that it won't be till January that I can leave (because the judges don't work over Christmas according to boys inside). That looks weird and hope it won't happen, but if it does then you'll come here and we'll be together and find our house and get into the Good and get my business going here. It feels good to me and I know it'll work and now I'm really anxious to get it on.

Lawyer gave me 20 Bs. which is now gone cause had to pay back some bread, but I'll be okay till tomorrow. Not gonna eat today anyhow (just juice and 3 chocolate bars which cost me 10 Bs., boy it can be expensive to live in prison unless you don't eat -- which is certainly where a lot of these guys are at.)

Lawyer said he didn't know about the letter that claimant signed withdrawing charges which Arthur gave to Interpol but I told him about it already and since it's the original that is only admitted as evidence it's important other lawyer has original of claimant's document and that he's appearing Monday in front of judge to have copy certified. That shows it's the original copy. Then it's okay. I go in alone to give a statement with a translator -- lawyer can't be present (crazy, huh), so I hope all my testimony is straight. Wish I could talk to my partner but I don't think that's safe. Hope he sends a letter outlining his statement and what else is important so I can be consistent. Altho at Interpol I said I didn't recognize the papers, etc., I can say that was because of my heart attack and concussion in the motorcycle accident (while surveying the land on Margarita) and my memory has been bad since then. So that's how it stands now and at least I feel I know a little more although it keeps changing and lawyer says I had bad luck. First in switching cells because of weekend and second cause original judge was sick this week and new judge didn't want to take case because by the time he studied the papers he'd be gone. The original judge will be back on Monday and I'll see him. It's possible this 8 days and 8 days thing is Friday; the original 8 days was up (first 3 days count or not?) on Wednesday and lawyer was before judge then, so on Thursday 8 days up even though I'm here only 6 days on Wednesday so that's why Thursday is Liberty Day -- it's confusing as hell and the answers always seem to change but I feel it coming my way now and at least I'm clued in a little. Even if I get out Thursday and can't go to N.Y. I can at least talk to you and we can get it on that way until we see what's happening with the investigation so I can go home. Everything here is time and patience and being cool until it happens. So I'm learning to have patience and I hope to really turn this experience into a benchmark for myself, coming on with a good head and "heart" and going forward from there...no more looking back. We've got our lives to look forward to...together. Dealing with everything with a cool and mellow smile cause that's the way to go. I Love ya so much I can hardly believe it but "trials by fire" is one way to find out and this is sure one of those. Here we go My Love, Hang on. Don't leave me in your body your heart or your soul. I'm coming soon.

It's two-thirty now and I had a few cigarettes and a chocolate bar and bullshitted with my friend Pedro. Here, if these guys are your friends they really go all out for you and everybody I've come in contact with so far has been groovy and some of the bad faces here I smile at and they say hello and no one is hassling me. I've got friends as they say and they really let me know it all the time, on the good side, nothing bad. Hope it keeps up that way. So I hope to be able to consider this my "cooling out" and "writing vacation." "Que Vacation!" Like an alchemist I intend to turn the bad into good. "Hang in there everybody -- I'm coming home soon." The guys here are really comin on groovy and I get all sorts of goodies (as per right now), joints all around and nose-candy as well. Good for energy and "starting the Heart" -- a la Norbo, and it goes on and on. I've been trans- lating a Spanish notebook -- a person tape me, we walk or do a joint and talk and I return to my chair -- another tap and repeat of another joint and conversation. So it's getting to be groovy under the circumstances and I'm feeling much better. Would love to see my partner here but I guess that'll have to wait until I'm out -- (a lot of things will have to) -- but I'm working out 3 times a day now and beginning to feel and show it. Studying and reading and relaxing from physical and mental fatigue. Still can't really

rest yet but I'm improv- ing and should be in shape to do so soon. Oh so soon, my love (this is the longest let- ter you've ever received or I've written and we're not likely to ever forget it).

Maybe this is the start of my writing again, I hope so -- a novel, a paper, a what-not, I don't care, it's good good therapy and it tells me so many things about me and the way I think and hang ups, etc. -- it cer- tainly will have good effects. Above all you'll know what I think and have gone thru so it's "ours" again…sharing and loving like we're supposed to…Love You.

═══════════════

They're eating and coaxing me but I'm not going to eat today…just juice. Feeling good, writing fast, it's coming. Outlining Yoga Exercise Plan next, then Meditation.

Well, been buzzing back and forth between one cell and another, came back and working on Spanish again and Ernie insists I eat so I'm eating some spaghetti. One of the guys from the next room came in and saw me and nearly passed out! Next thing I knew Todd came in to see me and said, "Quick go in and see the Americano eating." So I ate and have been reading Spanish comics and papers with my 'lil red dictionary at hand and just got hit by a 'candy' in the nose and a joint in the mouth and am feeling fine and mellow. Tomorrow is visitor's day and the floor was just waxed and beds made. Tomorrow's Sunday and it should be crazy cause these guys will have food and everybody comes in to the rooms (cells) and it goes on from 8 till 1 and then exhaustion. Everybody's shaved, we just had some sugar water; they're playing dominos on my floor-sleep-spot, someone spread newspapers on the floor and three drop-outs are asleep. I just asked Smiley how about the room service! Here we go again. What a shower! But checked out front and no no go. So I'm here again and smoking a cigarette -- get ready for round 2. Will cool out for awhile and the pen goes on. Listening to the sounds of the radio, the icebox being emptied to drain, and the dominos hitting the floor, and above all the constant sound of voices. It never stops here except at nite. Am going to the other part today, just waiting to visit the wrestler and the craszy and lay some goodies on them. They're

going soon (next week but you know what that means -- whenever!) but I made them smile before and tonite the sharpshooter said we could go there for 1 - 2 hours in the afternoon if I waited. He spoke to Chief -- I said thanks, 10 - 15 minutes is fine. It's all okay and they're nice cats. Place here is beginning to take form and I recognize the danger spots. Am going on to get the mostest out of it and digging what I can and the pen keeps going and so does my feeling. We're both so disoriented living in all these different worlds but it's coming together now. Not that we'll live in less of them, we'll just groove more in all of them.

So the cool's extending! It has to cause 3 guys were just brought in for dope and given a lesson upstairs -- Head Legs and Body -- some example! On the devil's lair floor -- the place where many go in and a few come out sideways every week. Some number. So much for the danger and back to you. The world's changing fast and so are we and that's what's both good and bad; but the idea is to open up all the valves and let the energy and communication pour in and let loose and glide with what's happening. The pace is our own, either adjust to it and like every other such thing it comes to be normal and slow, or otherwise it's too frenetic.

A bit paranoid about writing in this book. Afraid it might get taken away or what not. Be glad when Arthur's here to take 2 of the pads away.

The up sounds of music -- jazz-rock-black soul and it keeps going and changing the cultural number and reshaping heads, ideas, and the flow of things. MUSIC IS THE FORCE. The universal communicator. Everybody understands it and that's what to get to next. The world will see us yet -- the trip's just starting. Now is the real word. I'll be there soon. The music is getting to me…I'm writing and singing. More dropouts. The game's still on and someone is still walking around with a radio playing some guy

-- Roberto Carlo is his name -- "Magnifico!" And now Black Rock -- up temp -- Yeh! HA - Ah Now "I FEEL FREE," a Rock Group. Some slogan! Some Room Service! Some Vacation! Come play with ME -- FREE FREE FREE WITH ME.

Lucky 3. If I leave on Thursday that's the 7th of Dec. -- Pearl Harbor Day. The sinking of the old life and the start of the new. It goes on: the music, the sounds, the game and now the wrestling, the goosing, the boxing, and me and the writing. I'm beginning to understand the radio, watch out Venezuela -- here we come! Come here my love, come start a new life with me. Everything is ours. Taste it, it's here Now. No more false starts, this is our number; our time to get it out. Music of Maricaibo, the walkers go by, the dominos rattle, the change is counted and the dropouts dropped. I'm gonna take a shower and feel good and Oh Feel Good my Love. All's well that ends well. Here I Come. Bottoms up and the end is well and it's just the beginning. Now only Now, grab on here we Go GO GO GO my beautiful one but come back to me now now Love Len.

Sunday. It's six o'clock and I'm writing on the table where my sleeping spot was. 2 guys already out to work. I'm shaved, showered and dressed for the day (jeans and Zubin's tie-die sweat shirt). I'm writing away in the dark since the others are still sleeping cause they shaved last night and still have an hour before they have to get up. Got up like a shot and will do some exercises now and then pick up pad again. It's the 3rd of Dec and 3's my number and I love you like mad cause you're my number. Good Morning my Love, hope you're cool, I'm a comin. Love to all and everybody. The day starts...the sun's coming up. Hooray for us and all we love! Hi ya AppleAxe.

Gonyo, that's it for the exercises (15 minutes), too nervous in the room -- the people in bed are beginning to stir and the voices in the room are getting stronger. My lip (from motorcycle accident) is very stiff this morning and tingles when I exercise it. Oh for a good morning fuck…hours on end and then you guessed it, I won't go to the Baths -- not after that one! I got off, did you? Wonder what you're into; if you've gotten into some other cat or anything -- when I think like this I get crazy so I'll stop. Just be Happy and I'm with ya but just be there when I get back. Or else I don't know what cause I got a lot going on you and me -- this last in way of prayer. Anyway I love ya like "I never loved anybody" and it's NOW -- God knows what happens tomorrow. Get ready here I come -- Love Me Apple!

The Yoga really makes me feel good and I can feel my body vibrating with my stronger heartbeat as the blood runs thru my veins. My eyes are getting better, even with all the reading and the poor lighting in here. The sunlight never really comes in directly, just reflected rays.

The noise in hall is intensified as the clang, clang, clang of the mess hall is droning on continuously. Boy I'm glad I'm out of that other section. Wonder if my mother senses something wrong like she always does. You Mothers You…all of you I love ya…you lover you. I need you and you mind blowing tripster. I'm on my way. So the bedecked Arab Turban writes on; watching Smiley jump up and down, naked prick flying up and down, smiling and happy. What a place! It's all very disorganized but move a pencil and someone knows cause there're so few possessions that they're constantly being counted. Stalag 17 -- No! But Weirdo 2 -- yes! Sure is weird here with one minute peaceful and you can almost adjust and the next violence like last nite (wow). Who needs it -- but alas here I have no real choice except a drastic one, which I won't take cause my thing ain't that serious -- but I can see how you can easily flip out here. Some guys been here for years, have the jobs and concessions but for sure must be nutso by now if they weren't when they arrived. But I expect to be out this week, Dec 7th latest and if I don't, well then they charged me and for fraud it's 1 - 5, so what does that mean? For sure just stupidity and no-communication got me in here, and that'll never happen again. I hope that that's so and there's no more dues after this for anybody I love. But we all make mistakes and that's what makes the world go round. Ah, the light is getting better...I wish I could see the sun -- I really miss it. But in the end it's all our own trip; I chose somehow to be here and acted in a way to get me here. Mistakes are just part of the format for human endeavor and within the format in which I operated my exposure was great cause I wasn't in control of the events, at least in so far as even knowledge of them is concerned. A dog just barked and I miss the Dug and Sam and the Kiddens and Kats and You and the Kids and N.Y. and US...yes mostly US, cause you're like an extension of my feeling mechanism. When I think of you I get this love rush and it takes me to another place every time. But we have it so I'm not complaining. Far from it, it's just the separation and not being able to talk to you, let alone see you that's terrible. But some I know and love have it a hell of a lot worse and I feel for them more than I ever could before. I Love You -- All. Let's all make it back together, one way, one face, one togetherness. It's all part of the game of life but shit I wish life didn't keep testing us. It's sure a swift bird in flight with winds and currents of unpredictable nature. This wind has taught me to fly if not straighter then stronger and with

the current instead of against it. Use what's happening instead of fighting against it. Jesus, I feel good right now, must be the words and the day -- a 3, cause I'm comin on stronger and feeling right about things. Even now imagine that I've temporarily adjusted (what adjustment isn't temporary) to this place and I better leave soon before I get into it here. One sure learns a lot by looking -- whether you want to or not, and here you learn things of a multifarious nature -- some of them good but a hell of a lot of it based on the words "Watch Out, Attentionia" and so forth. It sure increases the psychotic in your paranoia (fear riding rampant thru your soul). Bang of the clubs on doors -- it's reveille and in a minute "numero." I'll turn on the light now. Just tried to; it's on ceiling and you hit switch with a broom and bulb blew, wonder what that means! Oh for an ole Merlin "Once and Future King" to tell me what these Omens portend. I know "Watch Out" or it means "Soon to Blow this Joint." A guard just came in and place is starting to hum. Think I'll lie down for awhile and wait for the Bang of "numero." Blew my nose and it's black brown from the air in here and all the cigarette smoking (did a pack yesterday but only 2/3 myself -- it's hard to stop smoking here, everybody does and continuously offers them if they like you and then it's like turning down a drink at a business lunch if you don't). Boy the little things mean so much when you have so few things going for you, but in the end it's only you and you alone that is the determinate of how you feel and how, with what's happening you are -- no matter where it is or the circumstance or who or when. Altho for sure there are determinates of location, the reaction formation and adjustment; the over-all life plan and style are a matter of choice, although the overt choice is surely limited, the Head Trip is not. Oh for the Glass Bead Game…in Prison…or in a Hamlet, it's all the same…just 2-legged creatures on the Earth playing games with themselves and one another. We're all just here to help each other thru it, or as a reflection of ourselves and our strengths and weaknesses "Love thy neighbor as thyself." Just put some Balsano Aleseida on -- it's like Tiger

Balm, Ben Gay or both and the tears are streaming down from my eyes and my nose and sinuses opened up. Boy what a Rush! Could use something else and who knows -- "The Shadow Do"! Planes flying outside…I need some MUSIC. Turned on and danced my ass off…laughing and singing…"It never rains in California." Tell all the Folks that I'll be Back Home Soon -- Don't Tell em where you found me (Ha). Aha, the IceMan cometh and soon the visitors and the food arriveth. I'll eat today for sure -- it's like a Fiesta! What emotion! Roberto Carlo, "Amara Amado," is now singing a love song sweet and sad with rhythm and violins, et al. Now an UP tempo "One More Mile To Go." Boy an hour here is like a year or an instant -- no betweens. Now I'll get a little 'nose-candy' and get my "heart started" -- Norbo!

Well gonna say hello to Toddio and walk a bit and then the guests will arrive -- it's about 7:30. Need a hot chocolate, then I'm ready for anything -- almost. "One more mile -- It's easy to make." She's the one who's waiting for me -- Here I come -- Ready oh so ready, are you? "You walked into my party," early -- heart attack victim and alla girls faded. "You're so fine" -- you know my song's about you. I had some dreams, there was you in my arms…you're so fine, all mine. Bet you know I love you.

═══════════════

I t's 9 now; swept the floor, danced, sang -- visitors line is about ¼ mile long so it takes a while to get them in. Sitting around waiting for the action to start and also to get my "Heart started"! Soon and Up and Up and Away and the visitors will come. God but the vibes are wild -- everybody waiting to see a face -- the emotion, tears, babies, wives, mothers, friends and food (the constant of this castle of towers), and late exhaustion, eating and sleep. Am writing without my glasses -- feels good.

Miguel didn't give my camera and bag to lawyer so gave lawyer his number and hope all's gonna be well. Need more pads -- this is the last of small ones -- it's good to write. Just get hit by a nose # -- ah candy speeds the heart and adrenalin in the system -- como no! Yeh it did it, here we go, visitors day, Hooray! Len Axe.

Well Arthur came, nervous as hell, brought me a shirt but no books; said I should be out Thursday. Discussed everything but no messages from my partner. Arthur's foot was bothering him and so is this situation; said 'Ironmountain' called and was leaning on him (the anxiety of all!) and of course, he tells nothing -- just that I'm incommunicado, so you and 'Ironmountain' know nothing. I'm just hoping that Wednesday or Thursday is the day I get out of here. Walking up and down hall after Arthur left (he couldn't sit) and his leg bothered him so I told him to take off and I'll see him Wednesday outside, I hope). If investigation is finished and closed then I can go to NY if not I'll stay here till it is or until they do another number on me or whatever. I'm nervous as hell now just picking up on the other vibes, but gave Arthur 2 notebooks and he's saving them. Boy the time drags and I'm emotionally exhausted. Almost everybody's gone and soon also the food and the nervous din of talk, talk, talk (as ever), and maybe I'll rest or exercise again or whatever. I'm running out of words. Think I'll do something different but I don't know what -- only have 2 pads other than this and one is for Spanish and To Do, so I'm worried about getting more (Big Worry) but I'm sure that's no problem (what's sure) anyhow! It's Sunday, tomorrow the judge -- although my name's not on the list. So maybe Tuesday, which puts it off another day, but nothing to do but "hang in." Hope you're not going too crazy but I'm sure that's not so. Just feel my love...I'm a coming. Love ya the most. The Axe-man loves the Apple Annie.

———————————

Drawing, writing, studying -- what a vacation. Nothing to do but wait and wait and wait some more. Soon my Love, soon. Well on to my Spanish and will say hello next door and grab some food and then into whatever.

Dig the radio, has a 3 - 4 hours of the best of '72 Rock concert. Borrowed a radio from Ernie and listening. Read an 800 page novel in an hour about Beauty Pagents -- was the worst. Now on to Leon Uri's "Armageddon" with this pad by my side and Spanish dictionary and books. Today's a weird day and I'm feeling it. Did 2 more 'nose-candys' and the energy carried me thru. 3 sandwiches on rolls with a suggestion of something in it -- a little nutso here today cause when the outside comes in everybody wants to go out with it. It makes you crazy! I'm lying down

-- "Grateful Dead" is on now and feels like home -- miss you more than ever. Wearing down today but my chin is up. Love you, love you darling Apple.

Boy is today nuts, been listening to the rock with radio behind my head. Ernie came in and took it back. I went to bathroom a while ago and saw a razor on shelf and had a sudden flash to cut my wrists. Smiled... not serious...but am nutso today, body sweating and feet cold. Dominos being played, people walking in and out and the constant drone of voices. I bet 6 Bs. on horses today -- #3 & 9 in 3rd & 6th races, wonder if I'll win! Races just coming over the radio now and light bulb's above my head glaring in my eyes. Must be 5:30. Yep, it's 5:15 racing results and announcer coming in strong.

"Armageddon," an old WWII book written with the morality and sense of that time to the over 50 audience and completely a drag to me. The announcer just went crazy at the end of the race, 6 just won in the 3rd, 4th race over now and it's up to the 6th race. I'm racing through the book thinking there must be better to read but everything is a drag and not with it. I'm just out of it. May have to start my own cult of reading and writing -- me and you and ours -- sounds like a complete and self-sufficient group, but I know it can't exist alone. We still have to deal with others. Here is a prime example -- no choice -- just people; deal 'em in or deal 'em out, they're still here. Boy what a day CRAZY! Oh yeh! It's amazing how tuned into vibes people are here. I'm reading, dying for something to eat but have 2 Bs. left so can't buy shit and my left hand's on top of my head when a piece of chocolate falls into it. I turn and see Smiley walking away with that big grin on his face. Crazy! Still reading and I've had it. Police playing dominos on my right shoulder so I go into Todd's room -- no satisfaction. Walk the halls -- back to reading, writing and waiting. For what (To Get Out of Here)? Nothing I can do -- name not posted, I probably won't go tomorrow -- so it's Tuesday then Thursday and out I hope. Oh well, make the best of it. Don't drive yourself up a wall -- not these walls. Happened again -- guy just hit me with a taste of nose-candy just when I was thinking of it. Hope the Big Judge catches my cry "Get Me Out of Here!"

Lost all my bets on the horses and now Momma Smiley insists I eat soup (chicken), brown rice and octopus, vegetables and a cigarette. Feel a little better, it's 10 PM and been up since 5 or 5:30. Long, hard, active and boring day. Love ya so much -- Need ya I'll be out soon.

Been reading and it's okay -- reading and shitting and a cigarette and a joint in the bathroom. Same time as I lit up Smiley came in looking for toothpaste and I ran right into the shower -- COLD -- what a feeling! You'd have loved it! Out and into bed. I'll finish this and read and say Goodnite My love. Tomorrow is TODAY AND TODAY IS OURS ALL THE WAY. Good nite to the Apple from the Axe.

━━━━━━━━━━━

Did a joint in dark and sleep came. Woke up early -- 5, and now is 6:30 - 7 and don't think my name is on board for Judge -- will go out and see now. No, my name not on list. Guess it'll be tomorrow and that conversation Arthur heard about Tuesday was right on, it will be Tuesday. Wonder if the lawyer will show to tell me what's up? 50/50 chance. Haven't a Bs. now and will cool it for the day on cigarettes. Nope, Smiley just threw me a pack. "Tuned in vibes"…a lot of brothers here. Some on same charge, others on different ones -- some like it here -- must seem more like home to them. Gonna read now and see if my name goes up at the last minute (doubt it). Was a drag to shave tho and not have to. I'll take a shower later when it's warmer cause I have a sore throat and no towel. Oh well that's my big problem (Ha)!

Two cigarettes and 3 hot chocolate (small 6¢ each) in morning. Cig- arettes making me a little dizzy; nice to lie in bed, spinal cyst acting up tho, feeling okay. Guess I needed sleep yesterday in addition to vibes. Adage -- "When in emotional slump sleep it off!" Feeling Good…that's good! Reading, will eat -- Smiley cooking. Boxer kissed Smiley on neck. (They never stop.) I laughed -- it's absurd. Kissinger and Lo Duc in Paris (when will they end it?) They say 2 weeks -- it's like being here! Lawyer says Wednesday -- doesn't show till Saturday. Chiefs say Free Tomorrow and I'm here 12 days plus 3 at Interpol. Oh well, name not on list today. Did a joint; it'll be there tomorrow. Feeling good and I kiss you a Beautiful Morning. Hello, I'm alive and well (Oh well - ah) in Venezuela! I Love You. Len.

Patio time -- everybody has to go -- the head of cell here got mad at guard and guard locked us in. The chief of floor (in a suit) came in with all the guards. I think he's complaining about the way the guard talked to him (they must take care of things here to come on so heavy). Loud voice, yelling, really mad -- like a Big customer staging a complaint against an employee in a Dept Store. Tried to find out what happened but no one wants to talk about it now. He wears (head of cell) knit underwear and combs his hair constantly, thinks he's a lady killer. Now he's moving around fast and almost strutting in his self-righteous indignant fury. But he's been great with me and in spite of the fact that the best of them are like constant children I dig 'em to a point. They fortunately all dig me. That is to say the Big Guys, the others are shy of me. It's okay this morning, we're locked in but I'm relaxed waiting to eat -- reading and writing. Got off the Bummer. Waiting to see if lawyer shows -- waiting to see if I go to the judge tomorrow -- waiting -- waiting. They play the same songs alla time (like the top ten numbers in the 50's &60's) 70% American, 30% Venezuelan.

Well, the argument was cause the guard locked the cell with no personal order. This cell is the envy of the whole place -- chief knows director and is upstairs alla time. We don't eat in dining room, eat here because of him. "The guards have small minds says he." Breakfast lining up -- bacon or something like that and I don't know what. My self-portrait looks like George Washington -- showed Chief pictures cause he started to read what I was writing. Breakfast of cereal and arrepas in it and mil, and a Danis (Yes, a Venezuelan Danish). Smiley really a "poco loco"! How come I'm always with and dig the crazys? (As if I didn't know!) I love you "crazy Apple" (sound like an Indian name) -- you are a "wild Indian" -- my babe and I love every minute of you. I'm coming soon, soon my dearest love-Apple.

Been reading and just had lunch at 2:20 of soup, 2 slices (small) of beef, and some rice, and a Pepsi (my return to eating), but it's really been 20 days without so I decided to turn it on a little! Smiley's like a mother forcing everybody to eat and eat more. I did and he's crazy-happy! Well, No lawyer. It's late afternoon 4:30 and so I'm gonna see what happens tonite when the list goes up. My name should be there and I'd be out Thursday -- the 7th. I Love ya. Gonna go take a corridor stroll and visit and read some more.

━━━━━━━━━━━━━━━

HEY I'M ON THE LIST FOR TOMORROW. THE JUDGE -- THEN THURSDAY AND OUT! I HOPE. HOORAY AND YEA! HERE I COME. I LOVE YOU - MY LOVE APPLE -- I'M COMING SOON. I'm # 84 (8 + 4 is 12 divisible by 3) come on babe! and my name is listed as Jeonard Ira Axelrad -- is pronounced "hayonard", some name huh! Just did some Yoga for 30 minutes with cat that looks like Barry, showered, teeth brushed, turban on head, finishing "Armageddon" and then will take some juice in an hour and go to sleep. Early to bed -- UP at 5:30 - 6; to Judge at 8 AM. Feeling Oh So Good. I'll Be Home SOON Love Ya Apple.

Well, finished the book, pretty good but ponderous. Guy here (2nd old guy) looks just like my doorman at Horatio St. One of the other old guys left in a whisper, never knew his name, just disappeared. Well tomorrow is 2 weeks since they stopped and detained me -- should find out by afternoon from lawyer when I get out. Hope it's Wednesday or Thursday at the latest, and that the investigation is dropped so I can come home. I Love Ya and we've got a lot to do. One thing is for you to read this longest letter you've ever received in your life, I'm sure! I want to share everything with you, I Love you so much. Arthur gave me sun glasses when I told him we go out to court handcuffed to one another -- "What if someone sees you," Oh God! (what a problem). Get me out of here I say -- Fuck everything else. I'm a comin home Babe! See ya soon. Nite for now, I love ya sooo mucho -- Len the Axe and the Apple herself together always. Love me I love you! Lights going out 1 by 1 - 2 left. Chief in shower. Dig a joint, reading Spanish, "Future Shock" and you. Floating high…with you…I love love for all and ever.

Tuesday. It's the day! Almost 8 and the call will come in a minute to go. Was up at 5:30 and it's been a few hours. Heard shots last nite, and dogs barking. I'm getting ready to go. I love you oh so much my baby. WISH US LUCK. Here I go -- I'll be HOME SOON. Love ya Apple, the Axe.

Well, waited from 8 to 10:40; they took about ½ the 100 or so guys to court but I didn't make it. My 2 buddies from cell 33 were there. The wrestler was the only one of us that went. Am more than a little disappointed, but asked chief of cell to make sure I go tomorrow, which is visitor's day and very few go. Which probably means the earliest I could get out is Friday with Monday and forever lurking in the distance. Everybody there was nervous as hell. Soldiers with Tommy guns and handcuffs for all. I just feel this thing dragging on forever and ever, but just staying as cool as I can...nothing else to do. The cyst is killing me, hope it goes away, been eating past few days and maybe I should stop again. Saw a detective from Interpol and asked him to have the red-headed One visit me (he's the one who's got the camera and I don't know if lawyer got it yet). The way things go here, I doubt it. Well, you'll have plenty to read when I get home...I hope soon, my babe. I Loves ya alla time...the most and the best, Len.

Lying on a bed (slept on it last 2 nites, it's Smiley's and caught a bad cold...drafts), television set was just brought in and it's on. Radio is playing and guys are walking in and out and talking and God is it Bedlam! I notice I can't write as much anymore...I guess I'm running out of things to say...it's so repetitious here. Oh yes, turns out that my friend Roger Y. went to same school as Todd; he's older and he studied the Stock Exchange or something. "Small universe," as the saying goes. Just ate lentil soup and rice with octo-

pus and Pepsi -- ugh. I'm doing it to myself again. I'm anxious as hell to get out of here, and if I miss tomorrow I probably can't get out till Monday and that bugs me. No need for it, I hope lawyer shows up cause I need a translator there and if I get there an no translator then I'm fucked up again! So many things to go wrong and they always do. You can depend on that, but nothing to do but wait and wait and wait. Wonder and think about you all the time. You must be getting fed up by now; especially cause Arthur never gives out information and makes everybody crazy to boot, including himself. But he's been an angel here in this case and without him I would have really been fucked up. That goddamn testimony of mine -- trying to cover and not knowing what had been said already. Well, as the Jews say "Never Again." If I didn't have you in my life I'd be lost…more than I ever knew I Love you sweet, Sweet love. I'm coming soon -- Love ya, Len.

Well, new list is up and I'm 25th out of 43 in this section. Hope I make it, wonder if chief of cell went up to director for me? Good insurance. Tomorrow's visitor's day and Arthur probably will come. Boy is he fucked up with this whole number. I really feel for him, if he wasn't such a put-down on himself he'd be more than the confused groovy guy he is -- he'd be happy. Well, the Boys here knew -- not the lawyer, like he said. But that makes me not at all happy. Handsome (chief of cell) just came in and didn't say anything so I guess he didn't sound his friend the Director. I'll ask him again for tomorrow to make sure I go…or maybe not…see how it bounces.

Talking of bouncing, I miss seeing and dancing with you. Seeing those arms go out and shoulders drop, the slight tilt and turn and that apple-smile. Boy you really got me hooked! Love you in a million different feelings and moods, but mostly you're in my mind all the time and soon, soon I know you'll be in my arms. We'll love, travel, laugh, sing, dance and love and love and love till we are just love and all the pain and frustration is just so overpowered that it won't even be in our consciousness. Gonna do some walking. The hall is 30 yards long so every 3 times or so is a football field, or 30 - 40 times is a mile; so I'll go do my mile. Funny that the old guy here looks like "Bill" the doorman on Horatio St. The world's so big and so small, but I feel like a giant thinking that soon I'll be home and we'll be together again for always -- I love.

Well, sounded Handsome, and Todd dropped in and said that out of whole list about a 1/3 was taken today so I'll be taken tomorrow. Won't be long now for my performance and then out -- out damn place -- I go to my babe! Something is happening -- a guard came to talk to Handsome and he's packing his stuff for sleeping somewhere else, I think. The place is all watching and I'll wait awhile to ask what's happening. It sure don't have good overtones though. He's taking a mattress also -- wonder what's up. Always the smell of fear in the air and the littlest guard can turn anybody around with a paper slip with someone's name on it. Witness Handsome's scene -- who is the most influential guy in this set-up -- that's to say up to now. Looks like trouble. His brother is carrying his stuff. I WISH HIM LUCK WOW THE FEAR! Hope he's gonna be okay. Hope we all are. HOPE IS ETENAL -- I LOVE YOU -- HOPE YO'RE STILL IN THERE WITH ME. You have to be. Anything this strong has gotta be both sides. See ya soon babe.

It's bad, I just asked and no one wants to talk about it yet. "It's bad." Head shake yes. Hope it's not 'candy'-coated bullshit that they wanted to hang on him. He's been nice to me! Good luck, Handsome! Well, it was about that screaming at the guards yesterday -- they took him up to the 4th floor to teach him a lesson. Probably beat him up, the guys say, but his brother says no. I hope not. He'll be back tomorrow they say. Good luck, Handsome. Guard at my left shoulder looking at me writing so I'll sign off. We're watching television with glasses brought in by Arthur -- Old American Picture with Spanish dubs. Love and Love.

It's late now and I've got a bad cold. Tomorrow I go to court -- let's hope I'm out soon.

Watched some boxing on TV, read comics in Spanish and Spanish books, and thought mostly of you. I loves ya…keep in there…I'm coming soon. Len Axe Man hisself Loves the Apple.

It's Wednesday morning -- almost 8. Frenetic rush of visitors and I'm going to court. Love ya…keep our legs entwined…Love.

Well, 24 persons were there and 20 went, but no luck -- not me. My name was all alone so that meant a different building and different guards and a separate trip so it's mañana I hope -- Dec 7 -- Pearl Harbor Day, and I hope I sink this bullshit! Arthur hasn't shown yet and it's 11 AM -- 1 more hour of visitors. I gave a friend's sister my lawyer's and Arthur's number to call and tell them to get on the stick. Haven't seen lawyer since Friday and owe about 50 Bs. as of now (for laundry, juice, cigarettes and shaving, so he better show cause that's big money here). Everybody nervous -- these visitors days knock the shit out of you. Vendors all over (coffee, hot chocolate, souvenirs like crazy) a real circus, side-show. You sit and talk in one room or go to another, walk, drink a toddy (hot chocolate) and repeat it all over. I wish Arthur would come but he probably won't since he thinks I went to court, and that everybody would leave so I could at least lie down. Up at 5 and I'm exhausted already from writing an hour and a half and then the disappointment of not going to court, and then the interminable walking and waiting and boredom. Oh what boredom -- I've had it here already! Just have to make that court scene and the 1 - 2 days and I'm out -- I hope. Nothing to do but hang in and just hope you're in there with me. I love you so much I can't stand the thought of losing you. I know you don't know what's happening cause I know how Arthur is, but I'd give anything to hear your voice and be reassured and reassure you. I Love you baby, stay with me. I'm coming home soon soon I hope. Tons and tons of infinite love -- The Axe.

========

Well, Smiley's brother is gonna call my lawyer to tell him to come here today so I can find out what's holding things up (and to get some money), and get Arthur to fill him in. I don't think lawyer will show today cause he's got nothing further to say. But if I'm not out by Friday or latest Monday I'm gonna switch to another lawyer (who Smiley's brother knows no money necessary -- 1 day he says). Smiley's getting out this week or early next and he did the Big Murder but he's connected and calls me his brother and says he'll take care of me as soon as he's out if I'm still here. Todd says he is connected and I'm lucky I fell in with him. He took care of the guard so if I'm on the list for tomorrow then I'll positively go to court. Well, I hope so (note the word "Hope" is all over the place). I got to get out, talk to you, hear your voice, touch you…I love you. You're everything to me. Hang in Apple, I love ya Lenny.

———————————

Everybody shares, those with food give to others (I'm a recipient). It's limited to their own cell group but not exclusively. I have zip now and the boys who run the concession here said not to worry, just take what I need. It's beautiful, especially when you consider that you're dealing with people who are killers, robbers, etc. -- supposedly the worst of civilization! But human misery (being locked up) does bring some people closer together. Especially in the same group; cause it's here where the greatest danger lies to the individual, and unconsciously I guess they try to smooth things out. There's no explaining it in detail now, but it's a rare and fine experience with the aspect of death and violence always lurking in the dark shadows and providing the backdrop.

Just finished the chapter on "cloning" in "Future Shock" and we're really the last of our kind. I'm so glad I found you, you Apple you. I want to spend whatever time I have left with you…experience new and old highs, and love love love you with all my power. That is and feels like the best high I can imagine. I need you, want you and you'll know when we're together physically again. I Love You. I feel my body…my thoughts are on us. Here we go my love…have patience…don't split cause we're coming into "our own" old and new wonderful "Full Life -- Turned on High." Love is Eternal and will transcend all the crap if we hang in there together. Stay with it -- I hope you're feeling my messages. Love, the AppleAxe.

———————————

Was taken to another place on the beach or Big House; went up to second floor and Big Guy there told me to go upstairs and make myself at home. Did so and then some guys came around that I knew.

There were guys and chicks there and I thought it was Coney Island. One of the guys I knew, Tiny, took me downstairs and I watched some kids climb a wall to an adjoining building (which was a civilian one) and climb in a window and away. I wandered out on the beach and put my stuff down -- took off my shoes -- and then my mother came along. We went back to the Big House. The guy behind the desk stood up, he was a giant -- about 7-1/2 feet tall and was the Chief of the place. Gave me a few minutes to talk to my mother and I did so -- cooled her out and she left. Then went upstairs and Tiny came over and gave me a joint; that was quite a trip and I asked him what kind of place this was, and he said "The place to be if you have to be here." I asked if I could call you and he said sure. I did another joint from this other guy and some nose-candy -- there was a chemical in the candy and I blew it out and went downstairs. I didn't buy anything cause my friend said too much, besides I had no cash. Boys and girls crowded the halls, I looked for Tiny, he wasn't there. Looked at the walls -- books and a huge ceiling-high etching of City and Country. A huge kitchen (with colors like a fiesta) and looked at inscription on the wall and it said "Engineers"! Turned around to look for Tiny again -- some girl was in his place -- she got up and I started to ask her where he was, but she didn't reply. I heard a voice behind me "Leonard," and I turned around and woke up in my bed here. SORRY I DIDN'T CALL YOU in my dream but I've been trying to do that ever since I got here. I love you, my mother's probably worried and that's what came through. You, I can't reach except I jerk off every night when I can with you, and regardless dream of you with regularity. Funny how you had a dream and called me before I left to come home -- remember, and you said that we wouldn't see each other again. I guess this was the trip you felt, but worry not my love, I'm coming soon. Think I'll check the list, it's 4:11. I love ya.

Yep, list just came out -- I'm 57th out of 80 - 90. Gave a guard 5 Bs. for insurance that I go tomorrow. Smiley said give 25 on credit but I know cash counts here so I hope the cat does it for me. I'll tell Smiley when he comes back, he disappeared somewhere. Told Todd the dream and it was so real I'm still turned on. Oh, how I want to touch you, to fuck your ass off...I just know you feel me, even now, as I feel you... Hang in Apple.

My lawyer didn't show but I'm sure he got the messages -- one from a guy's sister and one from Smiley's brother. One should get through, likewise Arthur. Well I hope I make it tomorrow cause that's what's holding me back. Everybody says I should do the guy who started this but frankly I've got no eyes. I just want to get back to you and start again and hang in with you forever. Whatever we have to do, to do it -- that's what's happening. I know that if this doesn't work out here I'll have to start something else in the States (California maybe) cause from the looks of it I blew my other economic numbers in N.Y. by now, but I couldn't care as long as we're together. I've got loads of energy now. That's one thing this experience has done -- it's unleashed a storehouse of energy that was locked up in my bird. Its gonna come out good and I'll look back at this as my Venezuelan vacation experience. "Que Vacationes!" I love ya Apple -- Hear My Cry -- Don't Go Away -- I'm Comin Home -- Duggie Kiddens Kids Kate Apple I'm a comin. The Axe.

Well it's almost bedtime, ate a chicken salad sandwich and some juice, getting ready for sleep. Did my exercises for ½ hour -- real heavy head stand and all, feel good, been reading "Future Shock" after my shower, and now gonna read a Spanish comic to get off early. I'll be up early for a heavy exercise session -- got some juice ready for breakfast, hit the guards to make sure I go to court and will hope to check out the supervisor with same in the morning. There's a big hassle over a missing pillow here and I had to insist heavy on my two. My name is spelled right for tomorrow -- 57 of 147 now -- so that's a good sign for superstitious me. I'm a tellin' you again and again how much I love you. Do ya hear me? Bon Soir my Love -- Till we see each other again, I love you the moistest -- long live Apple and the Axe, Love Love Love and "more" Love Me and You. PS. I'm on the floor again -- the guy I thought was a cop last night is a cell mate (maybe -- if not a cop), and the chief is back after one night upstairs. I'm glad for him. I'm going blind with this light but have to write; should have mailed you a letter but that Arthur didn't tell me till last Sunday he didn't really tell you where I was and what was happening. Hope you're cool. I'm down to a ½ pack of cigarettes a day, but my snot is black from the nicotine -- wonder what my lungs look like. Have been doing a lot of deep breathing and walk a mile a day (55 times down and up hall). I Love you babe…hang on…you've got a love book to read. We'll make it, I know we will. Love and more love, Lenny.

Pearl Harbor Day -- Dec 7th 1972! Here we go (I hope) -- it's after midnight; getting whistles for my red Brazilian bikini and watching the movie shit on TV. Here we go -- Come fly with me -- I Love ya The Infinite -- The Axe.

Morning. Well the moon shot didn't work. I guess I dropped out when the second countdown was stopped, so I guess fuck-ups can happen anywhere. Then when everybody went to sleep I woke up and couldn't fall out for 2 hours or so. I did myself up twice thinking of you. I hope you felt it. It's now 5:30. I just shaved, etc. to beat the rush at 7 when I'll do my exercises and then grab a quick shower before I dress and try to go to court. But today I'll make it cause three's my number and this is the 3rd try -- Come on Baby! Be my lucky 3. For you and me. Now I'll fall out for an hour or so and then the day will start again. I love you. You're my apple and the Best. Kisses…Love…and Fucks…Later.

Well, exercised, showered, and now my walk and hot chocolate, and off I go. Good Luck to us baby…come on Lucky Lenny, I Love ya…Apple Axe…Lenny.

HOORAY WE MADE IT!

2 PM. Well, I'm back and I made it. For a while this morning didn't know whether I'd go cause I'm a special trip -- solo, but I had taken care of everyone around and I ended up heart beating and handcuffed to another cat (black) seems like they're my brothers in pain. Got on this bus and drove into the city. Got off; guys in uniforms with Tommy guns guarding us and people watching. Went upstairs and sat on a chair -- half-hour passed and my lawyer came with my partner Richard. He said I'd be out this afternoon or tomorrow morning. Richard filled me in on business and the tempestuous discussions with you -- said you'd thought I was dead or I would have cabled. Well being here was like being "one of the living Dead." Then went in and gave 3 hours of testimony, with translator and straightened out my other testimony (which I didn't have to give, I'm now told). The guy at Interpol got pissed at me. He could have dropped it but said I tried to make a fool of him by saying I didn't know anything so he sent me to jail to teach me a lesson, where I couldn't be reached by my friends who seemed to have tried everything possible. Then the Judge was sick and the guy who took his place was a hard guy so it got kicked over to this week for the regular Judge. My partner went in after me at 1 to testify and this afternoon the Judge will see the papers and rule -- so today or tomorrow. But -- new catch is tomorrow's a holiday and I might just be kept over the weekend -- till Monday. Richard had no bread; he just gave the lawyer 2,000 Bs. so he gave me 5 Bs. and I borrowed 20 Bs. here from a cat I'm teaching Yoga so I can catch a cab and check in at Hilton. (Smiley's brother is the Asst. mgr. there, except he's on vacation). After this Judge rules it takes another Judge to throw out the investigation -- about another 7 days, and then home, and you. But as soon as I get out I can phone you and talk to you my beautiful love and soon we'll be together again forever and always. I love you so much.

———

Just ate some black bean soup. (Smiley insisted for a celebration. He's getting out soon too). Todd just came in and started to draw on the pad in the back and then just flashed off again. He'll be back -- in and out -- up and down. Noisy and music (superstar playing) and activity all day long. Oh for some peace with you. Crazy Arthur never told Richard to read my special notes to him at the end of each book so I could know what was going on. Poor nervous crazy Arthur. He's been great as far as he goes (this jail trip brought back memories of his days in a concentration camp) but thank goodness it's soon over and I won't have to ask him for anything and vice versa. I can imagine the conversations with you and Howard (good old Ironmountain) but he's come up with bread and one of the hard conversations Richard had with you was for his benefit. He says don't blame him too hard; funny how I like my friends to like one another! But anyhow, who cares as long as I got out of here and we're together again. I love you, baby. Hang in there…the Axe is Alive and Well (Oh so well) in Venezuela. You're always in my thoughts and I know you can feel me just as I feel you. Here I come…soon soon soon soon Love ya Apple. Axe.

Well it's 5:25 and so it doesn't look like tonite or tomorrow (cause of the holiday) and I'm more than a little crazy because of it. So it'll probably be Monday if all went well with the Judge (and that's the way it feels to me). Oh the thought of having to spend 3 days here after I'm officially free really gets me. But I must be getting used to waiting and the unexpected (and adjusting to it -- "Future Shock") so I'm writing it off; besides I feel good -- just took a shower and did a joint and as Todd said to me "Whatda you care as long as you know when you're getting out!" I guess that's so only I desperately want to talk to you and at least spare you any more days of anxiety but we'll have to wait I guess. Lightning just struck out of nowhere and now it's raining and I have to adjust to that too, cause that will further fuck up the order getting here, even if the lawyer brings it over (which I hope he will but I doubt). He has to know about the holiday cause the courts are closed and what lawyer could fail to know what that means -- I hope Richard told him (50 - 50 chance). I shouldn't have stopped the translator from calling my lawyer after my testimony, cause you've got to do the same thing three times to get it done once here. So who knows? Just WANT OUT AND WANT YOU. Fuck it -- whatever happens we're gonna be oh so cool so soon) the lights have been flashing on and off every 2 - 3 minutes and it's semi-dark). Fucking Rain! Caracas, this dumb number and whatever! I'M COMING HOME…SOON…MY LOVE.

Well, anyhow I really feel I'm getting out by Monday and that's what I'm ready for cause I can't do anything about it. So I love you and

I can do something about that -- I'm writing like a steam engine and that's what I feel like now -- like a sprinter ready to leave the blocks or like that smoking rocket that didn't take off last nite! Music is blaring Black Rock Manana -- WON'T YOU TAKE ME HOME. Watching one of the black guys draw -- he's the one who sleeps next to me -- quiet, never says anything but we smile and trade comics and cigarettes. He's got a real sharp pencil and is drawing the outline of a leaf. He's beautiful…an Aquarius… the 9th of February…his name's Jesus Maria Echenigue. So I'm just about to read my comic again and wait to see if the order shows (could come up to 9:30 tonite -- ha ha). Keep yourself together baby -- fireball Axe is coming Home and in shape for you -- "real Fine and Good." Oh so good for you and for me -- Bless ya I loves ya.

Odds just went back up. There is a court open tomorrow ("Instructional Court" -- whatever that is), so there's a chance that the order will come cause some messenger service of the courts will be working (I hope). At any rate this info comes out in dribs and drabs and I have to act like a prosecuting attorney to get at it, but a new list just went up for tomorrow and now everybody (experts included) think that I'll get out tomorrow -- assuming no fuck-up with the Judge, that is. But I feel real good about it and I'm flying high. I'm a gonna speak to ya soon soon by babe. I luvs ya mucho mucho and the muchoestest -- The Axe Lenny.

Well, had everybody looking for MY COMB, then I found it. Did that 3 times here!! Watching tele "Don Camillo" in Spanish (Oh my head hurts from all this foreign language shit). Well caught a bad cold from the floor and it's terrible at night. Took a shower and the draft got my body (oh complaints, complaints) WHERE ARE YOU? "So anxious to get out." Domino game's over -- all the guys screaming and laughing. What kids! Think I'll walk my mile, see ya soon soon babe.

In room, nose dripping, getting ready for sleep. I'm exhausted and comin' down hard from the excitement. Tomorrow is the day I hope, and I'll speak to you as soon as I hit the Hilton. I love ya Apple, think on that and stay with me. I'm with you alla time. Love and more love to everybody we both love (animals too) cause me and you is the NOW LOVERS! Sweet kisses, sweet love dreams…I dream of us, AppleAxe.

Two guys were killed today by prisoners in the other Tower. That's the scuttlebutt here and generally it's true cause it has its effect of terror and violence on the sophisticates (Ha). A lot of guys here for killing their ole ladies but their other women (the wives) stick with them and visit regularly. 1 out of 3 violent crimes (the Big M); but everybody whose got bread gets out, otherwise they rot. They've got a lot of people to employ and it helps keep the staff active and growing. The make-work bureaucracy factor. "Quelle Vide." Big name coming in tomorrow -- everybody excited. The ex-dictator's chief of secret police caught in a big cocaine raid and he ratted or something, so gets VIP treatment! Separate cell in tower -- no one gets tough with that guy -- guards, officials or prisoners. So I say goodnite again sweet beautiful Apple of my heart. I love ya...happiness and love shall follow us all the days of our lives. Love Lenny AppleAxe.

═══════════════

No sleeping yet. There's been a minor riot of beds against bars and screams that sound like help for 15 minutes now and the guards ain't in there yet (2nd floor). Everybody here keeps watching TV (a travelogue of NY -- "It's not my problem"). Now they're yelling out the # of the cell -- still banging -- getting worse. Other cells are picking it up. "Que pase"? who knows! It's definitely from one cell -- now the voices are yelling like a relay race -- still don't know what's happening. Stuff flying out windows. Crash! Still no guard! (I'm feeling no pain did a joint but cold worse at nite, and scars are infected and painful." Yells worse -- guards wait till they die and then go in. Still banging -- it's a killing -- getting louder -- no guards -- ugh! Silence -- the TV's on Brooklyn. A lot more voices are still screaming -- getting worse -- no one too excited here. Just can't explain it. "Yell you sons of bitches, there's a man being killed here!" Still banging. Police whistles. Mirrors thrown thru bars. Men yelling at one another. Silence. Deep murmur of voices -- someone got it for sure. The

TV sound down. "Dad a dad a dah dah" -- singing on radio coming from guard station. "He got his throat cut." Lights out -- writing by TV light -- guys talking about it now -- desperate. Some last nite. Oh how I love ya...I'll be home soon...Len.

———

Morning. Friday is Here! Noise finally stopped last nite. TV went out and I did a joint and myself thinking of you and fell out. "Numero" at 5:00. Guard counted us in the sack so I slept late -- till 7. Now my buddy and I are gonna do a joint. He woke up when I came out of bathroom and said "joint?" I said sure, so we do it in relays. I hope that order shows this morning. Boy am I excited about talking to you and getting out of here. My stomach's upset cause I've been drinking some soda but that'll stop when I can get juice and I'm outta here. Gonna go do the joint and then exercise and shave and shower, etc. Just did the joint and ah, it's good in morning...thinking of you...I love ya. It won't be long now -- The Axe.

———

Did a short burst of Yoga but I'm too full of today to do them. They're scrubbing the floors again, God what anal compulsive people. Ah, Smiley just ran after a cockroach and killed it -- Good trip, cocker. Imagine what this place would be if there weren't these anal compulsives around. Just gave Smiley a page from this book -- it'll bring him luck I know. Lucky Lenny Rides again. I'm coming Home Babe. Smiley's brother is coming and maybe he can expedite my ticket and certainly set me up at the Hilton and then YOU BABE -- BE THERE AND BE GLAD -- NOT SAD! IT'S THE AXE! So beautiful and fine this love I call mine.

It's a beautiful thing this love I have for you. It gets me off as only love can and now as we're coming together again I shudder in excitement and that's why I'll NOT DIE. You're the fulfillment of my Life. "Will ya be my

Wife" Oh not You (I know how you feel about legal marriages!) -- Willya have my BABE, OUR BABE BABE. Me and you and everything -- BABE -- SAY YES YOU!" CATCH ME CAUSE HERE I COME. They just called -- my ticket's gonna come. Luv ya Apple.

———

Sending out the message now for Smiley's brother. I told him to check the court for the paper first and then come here. Well we'll see how it works or if the lawyer comes to get me out. But out I go if the decision's been made and it has been. SO SO I you. I LOVE YOU -- think about ya -- the love love SO LOVE SO -- tall -- you LOVE and I do Ya all time you you. A poetic musical game of chairs -- staccato or I can't make up my mind -- waiting on the PAPER -- YAAZAAAH APPLEAXE.

———

Well, I really got few complaints cause I'm looking at a guy who's working putting in the ice and he's only got 2 stumps on his hand for pinchers instead of fingers (must be 20 yrs old if that -- somebody did his hand up in here for stealing). Smiley's got 4 bullet wounds in him -- war and peace -- an the knife scars here would have made the Prussians look like amateurs. And many other things so I've no complaints compared to the guys that are here -- justified or not. Your mind holds the gauge -- I'm comin' out today or Monday and that's soon compared to these guys. Ah what sweet thoughts of you my love -- Ready-O-no-Apple.

———

Elton John just came on "Don't let me belong to myself." Do You Dance-Wit Me-Do You Do You Wanna-Oh Babe. Do You Wanna

Dance-I Wanna. Do You? Well been readin "the Hard Charges" (about Indians) -- Picture was called "Tell em Willy Boy Was Here." I'm halfway through -- it's 1 PM and no ticket. Got all afternoon tho, but I sure wish they'd get a message to me that the Judge signed release so I'd know for sure. Even if it's Monday. Nothing to do but wait.

———

Walked my mile fast in hall, everybody thinks I'm going crazy and they may be right. Watched them looking in the steam closets off the hall (cause they go 25 guys in their cells and no room to cook) -- and walked faster. Can taste getting out of here…lie down…read…write…exercise…lie down…think of you…go crazy…calm myself down and write and think. I think of the time of my heavy 'do-myself-in' trip when I felt sorry for myself and tried to lay down and die. NO MORE OF THAT -- I WANT TO LIVE SO BAD I CAN TASTE IT AND YOU (who is livin to me). A lot of fuck-ups in this situation so one more won't surprise me but I'm gonna do a little directing from here on in. Especially with my own life and not let circumstances just push me around. We make our beds…come lie down with me. It's gonna be fun no matter what happens. I really need you and hope and pray that you feel me (notice how I repeat myself). Oh well, a little more reading then I'll draw and WAIT some more and then Spanish and then think and write of you and soon oh sooo soon I'll be there with you and Duggie and all the people and things I love and then we'll move on. We've got lots of traveling and things to see and we're gonna do it and laugh all the way to a bed and back again. I love ya…Apple… Axe.

———

IT JUST CAME. I'M FREE YEA!!!

Packed and dressed -- waiting in room with 2 other cats to get final clearance. Release came at 2:30, right after I finished page 33 -- my cell# here! What a vacation! I love ya Apple and I'm a gonna be speaking to you soon…Oh so soon my love. We'll be together. Love Apple Axe.

The thrill of going is still low-keyed and I intend to visit here on Sunday to pay back some goodness and money -- Smiley hit me with another 20 Bs. for a cab. Good Guys -- 'Murderers and Thieves and Runners of Dope'. They were groovy to me and made me realize what friendship and love and consideration is to another person and mostly how glad I am to be alive and Free (at last) and to love you and feel the life run through my body. Oh Babe if you could be with me now you'd feel a rush…You'll see. I'm a comin home babe -- soon oh so soon.

Love is what makes it and nothing could have demonstrated it more than this 17 day Venezuelano vacation. I mean to tell you that's what keeps us together and keeps us going on with a smile in our heads and a cheer in our hearts. I'm a ready for anything now. Scared yes, but ready to do battle with the world of darkness cause I feel my light comin' on and our time is here. NOW -- is what counts as I see over and over again and we're gonna do it all (everything we want), and mostly ourselves. Love -- YES -- that's the 4 letter word that beats everything hands down. God am I excited -- soon -- am waiting for the final papers and my jacket and passport. Boy do I feel good! I can hardly wait to hear your crazy excited voice! Goose pimples all over! I love ya all over! I'll bet this is the first book you ever had written to ya…I love ya…Apple and Edward and Melissa and Valient and Big Momma and Patience and Treasure and Blanche and Sam and Oh my Beautiful Duggie Duggie. I'm a comin home to ya TOGETHER… bodies…minds…and souls…ever together. Needing each other to express ourselves in the love we can project and the happiness we can share and build side by side, standing, lying down, fucking, running, laughing in the sun or rain and dancing and Oh So High on Happy! It's Our Day! This is our new life…life together as one. Let's tune in on the Happy. Here it comes for both of us and all those we love. ready -- Here COMES DADDIO -- AXE Lenny. Whatever we call ourselves our souls know we belong together in Love Loves ya Apple. Your own Lenny AppleAxe forever.

It's 4:30 and I'm out -- Free! They gave me my passport but not my jacket -- have to come back tomorrow. Paid 5 Bs. twice as tips but nothing helps with these guys. But I'm out-sitting in a cab. Rush hour even looks great to me! We're going on the autopista -- Got fingerprinted again and just managed to get the stuff off me after 10 minutes. The last guy to check me out was a smiling handsome black cat with a laugh -- it's him I see tomorrow for my jacket and more Bs. of course. But who cares -- I'M FREE!! Oh the driving feels good -- no traffic here -- it's as if nothing can slow me up getting to the Hilton and calling you. I can hardly wait to hear your voice. I'm coming Apple -- Hang in there! It feels great to be OUT -- OH SO FINE!!

I Love Ya Baby and this book is finished. I'm on my way to the Hilton and in a week back to you -- but for now get ready for our Life Trip -- it's gonna be FANTASTICAGORIA and all the wonderful things that love can bring us. A Donde Va, AppleAxe? We Know…Love…Lenny. Be Happy Apple.

www.ingramcontent.com/pod-product-compliance
Lightning Source LLC
Chambersburg PA
CBHW051735040426
42447CB00008B/1140